Copyright © 2020 Derek Good & Craig McFadyen

Book design by Justin Oefelein of SPX Multimedia

All rights reserved.

ISBN: 9798640744965

Imprint: Independently published

# Contents

About the authors .................................................................................... 1
Introduction ............................................................................................ 2
Activity Categories .................................................................................. 8
Activities ............................................................................................... 12
    Acronym Names ............................................................................. 12
    Adjective Intros .............................................................................. 14
    Alien Customers ............................................................................. 16
    Antennae ....................................................................................... 18
    Bag Of Tricks ................................................................................. 20
    Balloon Burst ................................................................................. 22
    Bank On It ...................................................................................... 24
    Bears, Ninjas And Cowboys ........................................................... 26
    Blind Pictures ................................................................................ 28
    Bucket List .................................................................................... 30
    Bus Stop ....................................................................................... 32
    Car Observations ........................................................................... 34
    Catch Phrase ................................................................................. 36
    Centre Of Attention ........................................................................ 38
    City Facts ...................................................................................... 40
    Company Trivia Quiz ...................................................................... 42
    Concentration Memory Cards ......................................................... 44
    Conference Call Bingo ................................................................... 46
    Consider The Consequences ......................................................... 48
    Cute Baby ..................................................................................... 50
    Desert Island ................................................................................. 52
    Dice Exercise ................................................................................ 54
    Ducks In A Row ............................................................................. 56
    Employee Spotlight ........................................................................ 58
    Excuses, Excuses ......................................................................... 60
    Favourites ..................................................................................... 62
    First Impressions ........................................................................... 64
    Generic Sales ................................................................................ 66
    Get Dressed .................................................................................. 68
    Guess Who ................................................................................... 70

| | |
|---|---|
| Hackathon | 72 |
| Happy Hour | 74 |
| Hashtag Day | 76 |
| Headache | 78 |
| Heads And Tails | 80 |
| Help From My Colleagues | 82 |
| I Would Be… | 84 |
| Introduction By Association | 86 |
| Introduction Questions | 88 |
| Laughter Is The Best Medicine | 90 |
| Leaders You Admire | 92 |
| Leadership Reflections | 94 |
| Listening Exercise | 96 |
| Listening Quiz | 98 |
| Loose Meanings | 100 |
| Mad Hatter Days | 102 |
| Memory Test | 104 |
| Metaphoric Gadgets | 106 |
| Multitasking Myth | 108 |
| My Moment | 110 |
| Never Done That | 112 |
| Not My Job | 114 |
| Objection! | 116 |
| Paper Folding | 118 |
| Perspective View | 120 |
| Phone Pics | 122 |
| Plants And Animals | 124 |
| Poor Customer Service | 126 |
| Positive Response | 128 |
| Pressure Cooker | 130 |
| Proximity | 132 |
| Question Storming | 134 |
| Random Objects | 136 |
| Recipe For Success | 138 |
| Recognition Spot | 140 |
| Revealing Team | 142 |

| | |
|---|---|
| Rock Paper Scissors | 144 |
| Sales Stamina | 146 |
| Self-Disclosure | 148 |
| Silver Lining | 150 |
| Simone Says | 152 |
| Sketch This | 154 |
| Smiling Chat | 156 |
| Something In Common | 158 |
| Something's Afoot | 160 |
| Songfest | 162 |
| Stress Temperature | 164 |
| Sunglasses | 166 |
| Superlatives | 168 |
| Switching Sides | 170 |
| Synchronised Clapping | 172 |
| Team Scavenger Hunt | 174 |
| Team Storytelling | 176 |
| The Pointer | 178 |
| This Year | 180 |
| Three Truths One Lie | 182 |
| Time Wasters | 184 |
| Top 5 | 186 |
| Traffic Light Review | 188 |
| Unfortunately Fortunately | 190 |
| Value Apps | 192 |
| Virtual Charades | 194 |
| Virtual Fitness | 196 |
| Virtual Pictionary | 198 |
| Virtual Race | 200 |
| What One Question? | 202 |
| What's In A Name? | 204 |
| Where's Wotsit? | 206 |
| Whose Office Is It? | 208 |
| Word Builder | 210 |
| Zap! | 212 |

# Dedication

We would like to dedicate this book to all the leaders and managers keeping their teams motivated and engaged remotely and all the facilitators running training sessions over the internet.

# About the authors

The authors have over 30 years joint experience and have been designing and running training, coaching and leadership sessions for companies of all sizes and government departments in multiple countries.

The activities in this book have been put together based on actual used and proven activities that will give you great results for your teams and training sessions.

The activities have been structured in such a way that they are easy to find to suit your particular need, each activity is set out the same way to ensure consistency and ease of use and application.

Once you are familiar with these activities you can begin experimenting with them in different ways and morphing them to suit your needs.

## Some suggested areas you can use these activities for could be:

- Induction programmes
- Team meetings
- Coaching sessions
- Training sessions
- Team building
- Motivational sessions
- Improve communication
- Just having fun!

## We hope you enjoy these activities as much as we did.

# Introduction

## Virtual teams

When people work in the same department or group but from different geographical locations, they effectively work as a virtual team. Virtual teams that work well often comprise of people who are okay to work independently of one another. For most people though, a high level of communication is essential in ensuring the work is done well and that the cooperation needed between co-workers is easily coordinated.

People working in a virtual team can find the experience lonely. A good level of communication is needed. In the 'State of Remote Report' of 2019, two of the biggest issues remote workers reported as their biggest struggles with working remotely were 'loneliness' and 'collaborating or communication'. Simple practices like virtual tea breaks with co-workers can help to simulate the office environment. Ensuring there is plenty of communication as a team as well as between colleagues and their manager can help in fostering a unified feel. There are plenty of positives for remote working opportunities that include a saving in time and travel costs for the worker and the potential of a better work / life balance and flexibility of hours. However, the lack of physical presence can be difficult for some and knowing how to engage people can lead to improved productivity and a sense of belonging.

As more teams find themselves in a virtual space, it is important for leaders to adapt their leadership style to suit the environment. Just because staff members are no longer in the same office, it is still important to keep them motivated and engaged.

As a leader you will need to have a toolbox of skills and tricks to help you navigate through remote or distance leadership. This book is aimed at helping you engage and motivate your teams with tried and proven activities that are great for use in online meetings and conferences or online training sessions. With a variety of activities you will be able to keep your teams energized and focused on the task at hand.

It's not just leaders who may need to work with remotely-based employees, trainers using technology to deliver training over distance also need to adapt their style to ensure that their participants receive a great experience and that knowledge transfer is happening.

# What is virtual team building?

Virtual team building is just like regular team building, except you're not in the same physical space. In a virtual team building activity, each team member is on their computer and the team interacts using an internet-connected tool: chat, video conference, etc. Many traditional team-building exercises such as icebreakers and even team lunches can be adapted to accommodate remote workers or all-remote teams.

For trainers or facilitators using this book, there are obvious benefits to know how to run activities during training sessions. Activities help to reinforce learning points and break up the session. When done well, activities may be more memorable that the training material.

For the sake of avoiding repetition on the activities shown in this book, the assumption is made that for most activities, a reliance on the group setting of a form of video conferencing tool and an internet connection is used.

# Benefits of using team building ice-breakers for meetings

To help the team bond better, you can run team building activities. These are successful when emotional connections are made among the participants. When teams learn new things about one another, it helps to foster trust and shared experience. In many ways, the physical gap then seems less of a barrier.

The goal of this list of virtual team building activities and games is to help your organisation:

- Build trust among team members
- Increase the rapport and cohesiveness of team members
- Increase group productivity
- Increase effective communication
- Learn more about your team members on a personal and professional level

# Make time for small talk

When managing remotely it's easy to fall into the trap of only communicating with your team when assigning work or when there's a problem.

That's not to say you should be completely keeping communication short and to the point. You're also on a deadline and sometimes you just have to talk about what needs to get done and move on.

However, you also need to build rapport with your remote workers. This means getting to know them as a person. When checking in with them, take the time to ask how they and their family are doing and dig into their interests and passions. It's a simple way to show that you actually value them.

### BONUS TIP:

When chatting with your remote workers don't forget to say their name. "Remember that a person's name is, to that person, the sweetest and most important sound in any language," wrote Dale Carnegie in *How to Win Friends and Influence People*.

This book will give you a wide range of different remote activities that will help energize and engage your teams before, during or after a session.

### There are four key things to remember to implement a successful activity

- You must know what outcome you are going to achieve by using it
- You must know how to run the activity and have practiced it well beforehand
- You must know how to debrief the activity for it to make sense and formulate a link
- You must know how to show the direct link between the learning outcome and the training being covered for the group to get the Ah Ha! moment.

Just because you aren't standing in front of your team physically doesn't mean you need to do any less prep for a session. For some reason people seem to assume that running sessions online is easier than face to face. In fact it's harder due to the range of different distractions that could be going on, therefore you need to be polished and prepped as best you can be that includes knowing your activities.

# Tips on using activities

- Know the connection & result you want the group to reach
- Know how to run the activity clearly and smoothly
- Use your activities at the right time for the right reasons
- Plan your activities before your training - not on the fly
- Have more activities than you need for your training

# Giving activity instructions

When giving instructions it is vital that you are consistent on how you deliver the steps of the activity to ensure the group will follow you. If you are unsure the group will pick up on this and may impact on your credibility and their learning.

Time and time again we have witnessed leaders and trainers getting frustrated with their groups because they have lost control during an activity and had to repeat themselves over and over again (to the point where one trainer has been witnessed shouting at their group!) so the frustration of the trainer damages the relationship with the group and they will be less likely to want to engage in future activities.

Control is even harder when running remote activities when you have a wider range of distractions to contend with. It may be worth setting some ground rules before you commence a session so all attendees know what is expected of them. These might include such things as:

- No use of phones while in the session
- All screens must be on
- Everyone is muted when they are not speaking
- Where possible ensure they are in a distraction free area

# Simple instructions

When giving instructions we have to have complete control of the group. This is a habit that is very easy to develop with the group providing you are consistent with your instructions. Before you know it they will be following your instructions to the letter!

## When giving instructions to a group remember these points:

- Know exactly what you want them to do
- Keep it short and concise
- Confirm clarification before beginning
- Ensure control of the group by being assertive
- Give time frames

## Here are six easy steps for giving activity instructions:

- Get Attention from the group
- When I say go… (Load the gun) emphasize the GO
- What I want you to do is….(Give instructions) (Aim the gun)
- Any questions on that? (Seek clarification)
- You'll have about 5 minutes for this (Timeframes)
- OK then GO (Sound) (FIRE the gun) Make a sound such as a clap when you say GO

**If you are consistent with this approach you will find that people won't move until you clap.**

### For example:

When I say go I want you choose a colour then I'll give you your next set of instructions – go!

When I say go I want you in your virtual break out rooms to discuss the last topic and write the answers on a pad. Any questions on that?

I'll give you about 5 minutes, OK then Go!

# During the activity

Ensure that you pay attention to the group while running an activity; running an activity is not an excuse for you to wander off and do something else leaving the group busy! Observe and listen to the group and watch the interactions, identify any frustrations or confusion and step in to avoid any damage being done by them not understanding what to do.

By staying involved with the group while they are undertaking an activity shows you care about what happens and that you are not just using the activity to distract the group while you do something else or kill time.

# Debrief after an activity

**It is vital** that after running an activity you debrief the learnings that have occurred and link them to the topic being discussed. This will assist with reinforcing the learning and creating a memorable anchor for future retention and recall.

If you do not debrief after running an activity you may in fact hinder the learning you have been trying to achieve because the group may be confused as to why they completed the activity. Debriefing also helps the group express and discuss any internal feelings, outcomes or breakthroughs they may have experienced during the activity.

Failure to debrief an activity also can make it look like you are killing time or trying to 'pad out' your session. It's a fine balance between too few activities and losing the groups concentration and running too many activities and them appearing to be used for the wrong reasons.

If you always keep a few activities up your sleeve you can use them should your group speed through something faster than normal or you may need to swap out some text training for an activity to get a point across.

## The important rule here is flexibility.

# Categories

Running sessions remotely either as a leader or a trainer can be enhanced by using activities that make a point and energize the group to help the interaction and attention levels be at their optimum level.

The activities in this book can all be used for various situations which we have listed as categories. For ease of reference, we have created sixteen categories with icons. Each activity can be used for at least one of the categorized situations. Most activities can be used in multiple situations so will have multiple icons indicated. Although activities may be used for a selection of messages, be clear in what you are trying to achieve and focus on the primary message and purpose of using the activity.

At the back of the book, the categories have been listed again with the activities that suit each of those situations listed, so if you are looking for an activity for a certain situation, use the section at the back of the book as a quick reference guide.

We have defined each of the categories in this section so you have a better understanding of what the category is about and why the associated activities could be useful.

### Building Product / Service Knowledge

People that work in organisations should be familiar with the products or services the organisation provides. In order to build that knowledge, certain activities can be used to strengthen the participants' grasp of the information. These activities can be used to remind and refresh their knowledge of the products or services. In particular, the products and services can be used as the topics for the activities.

### Change

One of the many constants in life is change. Every organisation goes through change and nations experience world events and economic shifts which often impact organisations and their people. In some cases, change is forecast but the results are unknown. It falls on leaders to know how to interpret that change and prepare their people for what is to come, sometimes without knowing what the actual form the change will take. The activities in this book can be used to help people get used to change, understand their reaction to change and to prepare for change to occur. When people are more prepared to face change, they will ease through the change more easily.

### Communication

The basis for all organisations to work well depends on good communication. Sometimes so basic they aren't spoken of, good communication skills are essential for people to work well in teams, across teams and with customers. Miscommunication can lead to mistakes, lost productivity and issues with time management and repeat work. Activities in this category will help you improve communication skills and reduce errors related to poor communication skills.

### Creativity

In today's world, two of the most sought after qualities include creativity and innovation. Although some people possess these as raw talents, everyone has the ability to be creative. Using the activities in this category can help boost creativity in the participants.

When the brain is forced to work in new areas and exposed to fresh thinking, new pathways can be explored and created rather than just using the usual methods.

### Customer Service

Every organisation should focus on providing excellence in customer service. Even government departments have mandates to provide their customers with a positive experience. Activities in this category provide the participants with opportunities to explore better ways of providing customer service and refresh the benefits for the customer, the staff member and the organisation.

### Icebreakers / Shift Starters

When running remote sessions, it's great to be able to get people enthused about being there and energized in order to maximize the participation level. These icebreakers are great to use at the start of a session and most can be used even if the team knows one another or whether it's a new group. If the session is around starting a shift off as a daily check-in, then these activities are a great way to get the group motivated to start the shift. Half of the activities in this book can be adapted to use as icebreakers or short activities.

### Improv / Thinking on your Feet

Another key skill that is assisting organisations these days is improvisation skills. In most roles, the ability to think on your feet is required and these activities will allow the participants to step outside their comfort zones a little and develop these improvisation skills.

### Just for Fun

If you are looking for an activity to just energize the group and have some fun, then you can use these activities. Some of them may also have an inherent message and can be found in other categories but sometimes you may just want to have some fun and not want to have to draw a lesson out of what you are doing. Choose one of these activities to just have some fun as a group.

## Leadership

Developing leadership skills can often mean serious discussion so why not break up the session with an activity that can be used to drive home a point and energize the group at the same time? These activities have specific reference to leadership skills and can be used in training or coaching leaders.

## Longer Term Activities

The activities in this category will require more than just the time in the session to run. These activities will take place over a longer period of time. This may mean you instruct people before the session to do something ready for when the session starts. It may also mean that people have a whole day or longer to complete the activity. These activities can be a good way to stretch out the experience over an extended period and can help to engage the participants for longer and therefore create a lasting impression.

## Organisation Values and Image

The values of an organisation often sit on walls and are quickly forgotten by the majority of staff members. There may be the occasional review but in many organisations, these words are displayed but not often lived. The activities in this category can be used to help staff members internalize the values of the organisation and make them a more prominent component in their everyday work life. In addition, these activities can be used to help refresh knowledge of the organisation and improve the image staff members have of the company which translates to both inward and outward commitments of working for it.

## Problem Solving

Having the ability to work through problems and quickly find solutions is a great skill to develop. These activities help to hone those problem solving skills so you can use them in situations that require people to be more adept in that area. These activities along with creativity and Improv activities all help to exercise the brain into fresh thinking and 'out-of-the-box' ways of looking at challenges.

## Review / Shift Endings

A great way to check on knowledge transfer following a training session or team meeting is to run a review activity. This allows you to check whether the information has been retained by the participants. These activities are also useful to check on information gleaned during a shift so if you are running a check-in at the end of a shift, you can use one of these activities for people to share their experiences. These can be run anytime you want to do a sanity check on what you've been discussing. They provide a fun way to help solidify the learnings from a session.

## Sales

The lifeblood of an organisation is to have customers and therefore income. The activities in this category will help you to develop sales skills in the participants. There are many components to sales including objection handling, offering solutions, features and benefits and closing the sale. Use these activities to target specific areas you want to improve. If you don't consider yourself in a sales role or a sales organisation, consider the fact that sales is often wrapped up in providing great customer service. You offer something your customer didn't know about to help them have a better experience with your organisation or its services.

## Stress / Resilience

These days, people seem to be under a lot of pressure and are stressed out. These activities can be used to help people understand stress better and be more resilient. Resilience is the ability to bounce back after a setback. Knowing these skills can help people better handle pressure, reduce their stress levels and be more resilient.

## Team Building

Half of the activities in this book can be used as team building activities. Consider using these activities as a way of building team cooperation, team understanding and to build team trust. Although the activities may have multiple applications, team building could be the primary reason to run activities in the first place. You could get more than one message across while running a team building activity.

# ACRONYM NAMES

### OBJECTIVE:

A great icebreaker to start of a session with a new group or a group that is well connected. A great way to build team knowledge of one another.

| MATERIAL REQUIRED: | TIME REQUIRED: |
|---|---|
| Paper and pen for each person | 10 - 15 minutes |

### INSTRUCTIONS:

Explain that we are going to do a quick exercise to get to know each other a little better in our group. This is called Acronym names. I'll show you how it is done. We're going to write our first name in letters down one side of a piece of paper and we are going to assign a word that says something about us or that we're interested in for each letter of our first name.

As an example, if my first name was DAVID, this is how it might look:

D – Director (I am the director of my company)

A – Apples ( I love apples and try to eat at least one per day)

V – Very in to comedy (I love comedy and watch comedy shows whenever I can).

I – Iceland (I went to Iceland last year on holiday – it was amazing!)

D – Department Store (I love shopping and especially department store shopping)

Make sure the group knows what's going to happen and tell them to start. Give them a few minutes to come up with something for each letter. Tell them they can be creative – like V can be 'Very happy'. If they have multiple letters in their name – they need to come up with something different for each letter regardless.

If someone has a long name and they are struggling, allow them to shorten it – like William to Will or Samantha to Sam. Offer your help to people that are obviously struggling. When everyone is ready (have a time limit), one by one, share to the group.

### DE-BRIEF AND REVIEW:

**ASK THE GROUP:**

- Who learnt something new?
- What was the most surprising fact?

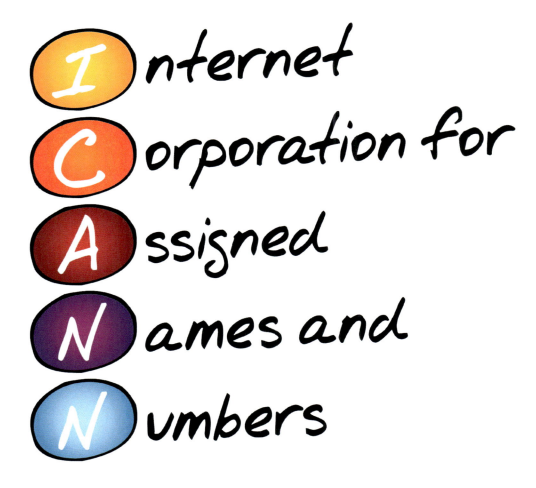

# ADJECTIVE INTROS

### OBJECTIVE:

A unique way to introduce people to each other. It helps to build team spirit by learning more about each other. Also ideal for existing teams.

| **MATERIAL REQUIRED:** | **TIME REQUIRED:** |
|---|---|
| None | 5 - 10 minutes |

### INSTRUCTIONS:

Ask each person to introduce themselves to the rest of the group by stating their name and also an adjective that represents one of their dominant characteristics. This adjective must also start with the same first letter of their first name:

Examples:
- Domineering David
- Sunshine-filled Sally
- Funny Freddy.

The person must back this up with an example or explanation behind their use of the adjective.

A variation for existing teams (although this could be a fun activity to do as described) could be to use the adjective to describe how they are feeling today or how their week has gone etc.

### DE-BRIEF AND REVIEW:

**ASK THE GROUP:**
- Who found that hard or easy?
- Who learnt something new?
- Were there a number of similarities?
- Was there some good diversity? How can that help us?
- What variations could we do for future sessions?

# ALIEN CUSTOMERS

### OBJECTIVE:

To help the group utilise their knowledge of the organisation to summarise and share with others. Uses problem solving skills and helps to adapt knowledge.

| MATERIAL REQUIRED: | TIME REQUIRED: |
|---|---|
| Paper and pens | 20 minutes |

### INSTRUCTIONS:

Put the group into smaller break out rooms for this activity if possible. You could run it as individuals but small groups would be good.

Tell the group that aliens have landed and are interested to know about our organisation. Normal communication is a problem as they don't speak with any familiar language. Ask the group to come up with five symbols or pictures that help explain what the organisation does.

Allow the group time to consult and come up with the image they will share.

Have the smaller groups share back with the wider group.

### DE-BRIEF AND REVIEW:

Look at the symbols and see what similarities were there.

**ASK THE GROUP:**

- What did you learn from this activity?
- What would you do differently if you had to do this again?
- How can we use this in helping us with our customers in the future?
- Is there anything we need to change in our roles?

# ANTENNAE

### OBJECTIVE:

A bit of fun to demonstrate ways we can be more aware of those around us and how we can work together better as a team.

| MATERIAL REQUIRED: | TIME REQUIRED: |
| --- | --- |
| 3 pipe cleaners (chenille stems) for each person | 10 - 15 minutes |

### INSTRUCTIONS:

Hand out 3 pipe cleaners (chenille stems) to each person and demonstrate fixing two together with about ½ inch of each overlapping and twisting round each other. Fix the third one in the same way to create one long pipe cleaner.

Put the pipe cleaners around your head and tie them together at the front and create two antennae. Leave the antennae on your head and encourage everyone to make a pair of antennae themselves and leave them on.

Ask everyone what the things on the head are. The name Antennae should come out pretty easily. Draw a line down the middle of the whiteboard. On the left hand side write "What are these for?" and ask for feedback from the group. Answers will include:

- Feeling, Sensing
- Checking boundaries
- Giving signals
- Receiving information

On the right hand side of the whiteboard write "What prevents these from working?" and as for feedback from the group. Answer will include:

- Interference / miscommunication
- Noise
- Interruptions, They break
- Switching off, No feedback

### DE-BRIEF AND REVIEW:

#### ASK THE GROUP:

- Discuss as a group how these findings can relate as a team, to customers, colleagues, managers, staff etc. Have them come up with ways to avoid the issues that may occur in the right hand column.

# BAG OF TRICKS

### OBJECTIVE:

This remote energizer is a bit of fun and also helps the group to work on creative skills. It's a way to get people to think quickly on their feet, be creative and learn that having something concrete in front of you helps.

| MATERIAL REQUIRED: | TIME REQUIRED: |
|---|---|
| Bag of items prepared in advance by you | 10 - 20 minutes |

### INSTRUCTIONS:

Put a few items into a bag and have them ready for your session. Items can be everyday objects like a tape dispenser, a candle, matches, a ruler, keys, a Lego block, a candy bar, a hat, a glove, a stapler etc.

Explain to the group that you have a bag of items and that you will be pulling out one item at a time. Assign one person to share how that item could represent something specific like "How does this item represent our business or what our business provides?"

Allow one item per person about the topic. You could vary the game by asking people to shout out what they think. However, it's a good way to get everyone to have a turn and share their thoughts.

Vary the question about representing as required. Other options could include:

- How does this item represent what value you bring to the team?
- How does this item represent what our competitors are doing?
- How does this item represent an issue we are trying to solve?

### DE-BRIEF AND REVIEW:

**ASK THEM:**

- What did we learn?
- How hard or easy was it to come up with something?
- Did it help that there was something physical to talk about?

# BALLOON BURST

### OBJECTIVE:

A great way of demonstrating how stress can build before an event even occurs.

| **MATERIAL REQUIRED:** | **TIME REQUIRED:** |
|---|---|
| Balloon and a pin | 10 - 15 minutes |

### INSTRUCTIONS:

Use a large balloon and a drawing pin.

Blow up the balloon in front of the group without saying anything.

Then tell people that you are going to pop it at some point during the meeting, but you are not going to tell them when.

Then you can ask how they feel and engage in a discussion about the different anxieties that build up before a person feels "stressed."

Discuss how what we imagine an event to be like can cause most of the stress before the event even happens.

### DE-BRIEF AND REVIEW:

**ASK THE GROUP:**

- Are there any events at work that build up stress before they even happen?
- What can they do as a team to help reduce that build up before it happens?

# BANK ON IT

### OBJECTIVE:

This icebreaker helps to start a session off on a positive note. It is useful to highlight how we all benefit from positive feedback and challenges participants to consider how often they provide it themselves.

The icebreaker is particularly useful in training sessions such as; Great Leadership Skills, Assertiveness Skills, Building Relationships, Emotional Intelligence and Leading Effective Teams.

| MATERIAL REQUIRED: | TIME REQUIRED: |
| --- | --- |
| None | 10 - 15 minutes |

### INSTRUCTIONS:

Explain the concept of the 'Emotional Bank Account' as follows…

"We all know what a financial bank account is. We make deposits into it and build up a reserve from which we can make withdrawals when we need to. An Emotional Bank Account is a metaphor that describes the amount of trust that's been built up in a relationship. It's the feeling of safeness you have with another human being.

If I make deposits into an Emotional Bank Account with you through courtesy, kindness, honesty, and keeping my commitments to you, I build up a reserve. Your trust toward me becomes higher, and I can call upon that trust many times if I need to. I can even make mistakes and that trust level will compensate for it."

When you are sure that participants understand the concept of the emotional bank account, ask them to introduce themselves to the rest of the group by stating their name and providing two examples from this working week that demonstrate how they have paid into the 'emotional bank account' they have with another person i.e. two positive actions they have made that someone else would have appreciated and logged. If they already know each other – this is still a great exercise to do for existing teams. They may gather some new ideas.

### DE-BRIEF AND REVIEW:

#### ASK THE GROUP:

This will start your session off on a high note and also show how important it is that we demonstrate positive actions to others. Ask if anyone is going to try something new as a result of this activity.

# BEARS, NINJAS AND COWBOYS

### OBJECTIVE:

A quick fun energizing activity.

| MATERIAL REQUIRED: | TIME REQUIRED: |
|---|---|
| None | 5 - 10 minutes minutes depending on size of the group. |

### INSTRUCTIONS:

Much like the classic rock, paper, scissors game, each player chooses between three poses.

- Bears eat ninjas,
- Ninjas beat up cowboys,
- Cowboys shoot bears.

Randomly choose people and set them against each other. Each player either roars for bears, shoots finger guns for cowboys or strikes a ninja pose.

The winners of each round go on to fight other opponents until you have decided enough time has passed or there is a clear winner.

This is a great team building game to get everyone to let loose and get a little silly.

### DE-BRIEF AND REVIEW:

**ASK THE GROUP:**

Discuss how much fun that was and how it got the energy going.

Remote Activities For Virtual Teams

# BLIND PICTURES

### OBJECTIVE:

This activity helps promote good communication and can give insights into customer frustrations with communication problems.

| MATERIAL REQUIRED: | TIME REQUIRED: |
|---|---|
| Pen and paper for each person and an image to view | 10 - 15 minutes |

### INSTRUCTIONS:

Provide a line drawing picture to one person and ask them to describe the picture to the rest of the group. They can only use descriptive words like 'line', 'angle' and shapes but not what the actual image is.

Each member of the group then draws what they hear. They aren't allowed to ask any clarifying questions or respond in any way. The person describing is the only one to talk.

When they are finished have each person reveal what they have drawn, then have the actual image displayed.

Any image could be used – here is a sample:

### DE-BRIEF AND REVIEW:

**ASK THE GROUP:**

Focus on what the experience was like considering there was no two-way communication.
- What was that like for them?
- How similar were the pictures that they drew?

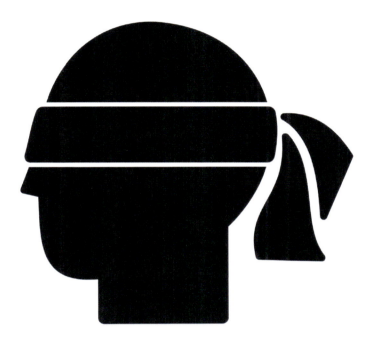

# BUCKET LIST

### OBJECTIVE:

To help groups understand one another and learn some of the motivators each has. Can be used as an icebreaker or team building activity.

| MATERIAL REQUIRED: | TIME REQUIRED: |
|---|---|
| Paper and pen for everyone | 10 - 20 minutes |

### INSTRUCTIONS:

Most people have heard pf a bucket list. It's a list of things people want to do or achieve before they kick the bucket (die).

Ask the group to write down 5 things they want to do before they die. Give them some scope if you need to. It can be anything at all. Suggest some ideas that people may have had – like travel to a certain country, run a marathon, write a book etc.

Give everybody 2-3 minutes to write down 5 things they want to do.

Have each person share one by one their list. Allow for questions or comments. If someone else has it on their list – have them say so. You could even turn it into more fun by having others shout out a word like 'DITTO' if they hear one of their items on their lists shared.

If someone has completed one of those bucket list items shared – have them shout out a different word like 'COMPLETE'. They may like to share what it was like to do that thing.

Ensure everyone has had a chance to share.

### DE-BRIEF AND REVIEW:

**ASK THE GROUP:**

This could be a way of getting to know people well. You may like to suggest those with the same goals to get together and discuss plans that they can individually achieve them.

Talk about goals and the difference between them happening or not.

# BUS STOP

### OBJECTIVE:

This activity is lots of fun and can help develop quick thinking skills, product knowledge and being more creative.

| MATERIAL REQUIRED: | TIME REQUIRED: |
|---|---|
| Paper and pen for each person | 20 - 30 minutes |

### INSTRUCTIONS:

For this activity, each person needs a piece of paper and to draw several lines to create a grid. Choose at least five topics that people will write at the top of the page (horizontally) and leave a space on the left side of the grid for a letter to be written in.

Topics could range from general interest to product or company information. For example:

- A product we supply
- A country
- A girl's name
- An animal
- Something in your office

Here's a sample grid. The letters would be added in later as you go. See further instructions:

| LETTER | A product we supply | A country | A girl's name | An animal | Something in your office | SCORE |
|---|---|---|---|---|---|---|
| S | | | | | | |
| D | | | | | | |
| E | | | | | | |
| A | | | | | | |
| W | | | | | | |
| T | | | | | | |

Once everyone has completed their grid, choose one player to be the bus and another player to stop the bus. The second player says go and the first player runs through the alphabet in their head. The second player says stop when they want to and the first player shares the letter they got to in the alphabet. Each player writes the letter down on the sheet and you start a timer for one minute. Everyone then has to think of a word that starts with that letter for each of the categories.

After a minute, share answers. A duplicate answer with another team member gets 5 points. A unique answer that no one else gets is 10 points. Zero points for no answer.

Repeat for the next letter until you finish the space and add up the totals.

### DE-BRIEF AND REVIEW:

Hopefully the group will have enjoyed the experience.

**ASK THE GROUP:**
- Did you learn anything new?
- What other categories could we do?
- What did this teach us about creativity? About Quick Thinking?

Remote Activities For Virtual Teams

# CAR OBSERVATIONS

### OBJECTIVE:

To illustrate that we can find the good or bad in any situation if we are looking at it and that we can make judgements and assumptions easily based on what we first see. Good leadership activity about coaching. Good to help negative people see the positive.

| **MATERIAL REQUIRED:** | **TIME REQUIRED:** |
|---|---|
| Picture of a car | 15 – 20 minutes |
| Pen and paper for each group / person | |

### INSTRUCTIONS:

Explain to everyone that we will divide into two virtual groups via breakout rooms if possible. Alternatively assign each person to be on a virtual team. Explain that you will be showing a picture of a car for everyone to see. Assign each group to either identify and write down as many positive things they can find about the car in the picture or as many negative things they can find. A group needs to be specifically aware that they are looking for only either positive or negative things.

Give the groups a time limit – like 5 minutes to discuss and write down their lists.

Have the groups or individuals share their findings with the rest of the wider group. Sample car picture:

### DE-BRIEF AND REVIEW:

**ASK THEM:**

- What did you notice about the lists of findings?
- How come we could find so many positive and negative things about the same car?
- How can we apply this to our roles? Giving Feedback? Managers?

# CATCH PHRASE

## OBJECTIVE:

A good way to test knowledge of products or co-workers in a fun and challenging way. It helps teams a gain a deeper understanding and can be a good training activity.

| MATERIAL REQUIRED: | TIME REQUIRED: |
|---|---|
| None | 15 – 30 minutes depending on size of the group. |

## INSTRUCTIONS:

In this classic party game, participants take turns describing words and phrases to their teammates without saying the word or phrase itself. Phrases can include celebrities, expressions, or even simple things found around the house. If my phrase is "needle in a haystack," for example, a clue I might give to my teammates could be "a pointy object buried inside farm equipment."

Catch Phrase is the perfect way to get your teams together and teach them how to communicate with one another. (Don't worry, everyone will be having so much fun, they won't realize that's what you're doing.)

Think about business or product-related words and see how well they can describe them to their co workers without saying it!

## DE-BRIEF AND REVIEW:

### ASK THE GROUP:

Discuss how easy it was to describe or guess the product or business related word.

# CENTRE OF ATTENTION

## OBJECTIVE:

A great icebreaker to use at the start of a session with a new group or a group that is well connected. A great way to build team knowledge of one another.

| MATERIAL REQUIRED: | TIME REQUIRED: |
| --- | --- |
| None | 15 - 30 minutes |

## INSTRUCTIONS:

Choose one team member to play the role of an employee who has been causing difficult situations such as missing deadlines, too many sick days, late for work etc.

Each of the other participants demonstrates a different style of leader to deal with the situation.

After each demonstration of how to deal with the employee, ask the whole group to reflect on the different leadership approaches. For example, the group could consider what worked and what did not.

## DE-BRIEF AND REVIEW:

**ASK THE GROUP:**

- Who learnt something new?
- Ask the group to consider what the 'ideal' leader would do in the scenario?

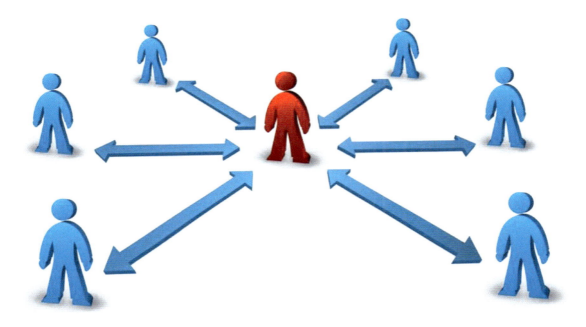

# CITY FACTS

### OBJECTIVE:

A simple activity to start off a session in order to learn more about each other.

| MATERIAL REQUIRED: | TIME REQUIRED: |
|---|---|
| None | 5 minutes plus a day's notice |

### INSTRUCTIONS:

Give everyone a day's notice to find a fun fact about the city they were born in.

At the next session, have each person share where they were born and their fun fact about their place of birth.

If there's time, you may want to suggest more than one fact per person.

### DE-BRIEF AND REVIEW:

**ASK THE GROUP:**

- Who learnt something new?
- What was the most surprising fact?
- What variations of this activity could we use for another time?

# COMPANY TRIVIA QUIZ

### OBJECTIVE:

A great way for the team to learn a little bit about each other and also a good way of testing company knowledge.

| MATERIAL REQUIRED: | TIME REQUIRED: |
| --- | --- |
| None | 10 – 15 minutes plus some pre-work time |

### INSTRUCTIONS:

You can create a simple trivia question before each team member begins to update everyone about the current project that they are working on.

Consider multiple-choice answers, as it is easier and faster for everybody to pick an answer instead of letting them guess.

While this requires some homework on each of your team members, as you would need to know the right answer, it would be worthwhile and exciting. You can also mix it up with company / product related questions as well.

**EXAMPLES OF QUESTIONS INCLUDE:**

- Personal related questions:

    How many children does Derek have?

    Which team member is allergic to peanuts?

    Which team member was born in _____?

    Which team member recently had a holiday?

- Employment related questions:

    Which team member has been with the company the longest?

    Who recently celebrated her first year work anniversary?

    Which team member has the highest sales?

    Which team member has the most compliments?

### DE-BRIEF AND REVIEW:

Discuss any questions that couldn't be answered and make sure you build in some company / product related questions to reinforce ongoing learning.

# CONCENTRATION MEMORY CARDS

### OBJECTIVE:

A good way to test knowledge of products or co-workers in a fun and challenging way.

| MATERIAL REQUIRED: | TIME REQUIRED: |
|---|---|
| Blank cards prewritten with matching choices | 15 – 25 minutes depending on size of the group. |

### INSTRUCTIONS:

Here's a professional spin on the 1960s game show. The original game show, called Concentration. Put 30 numbered tiles up on a board, each tile with an identical tile somewhere else on the board. What made them identical? They had matching prizes on the back. Over time, as contestants opened up more tiles, they had the opportunity select tiles they knew would match up and win the prize written on the back.

Businesses -- especially marketing departments -- can have a field day putting logos, slogans, and company names on the back of their own tiles and having players match up every piece of the brand. As your business grows, you can even put the names of your own products, employees, and job titles on the backs of your tiles to see how well your co-workers know the company they work for.

Try different ways of doing this by having staff take turns to call out two cards, if they match they win and the cards are removed if not they are turned back over and its the next person's turn. You will need to have the tiles shown on the screen or video on a board from the host.

### DE-BRIEF AND REVIEW:

Discuss what things were easier to remember and why, especially work or product related items. Highlights areas for further training.

# MEMORY GAME

Remote Activities For Virtual Teams

# CONFERENCE CALL BINGO

### OBJECTIVE:

To have a bit of fun on a conference all and practice being observant to what is going on around you. It also helps to prove the point that people will watch even the smallest things.

| MATERIAL REQUIRED: | TIME REQUIRED: |
|---|---|
| None | 10 - 30 minutes |

### INSTRUCTIONS:

Create some Bingo cards that you can easily email around. Make them slightly different for each person. Consider a 5 x 5 square paper or any size you think appropriate for the time. The game could last for the entire call or you could make it last the day depending on your requirements or technology.

Some examples you could use for the squares could include:

Someone saying "Can you hear me?"

Someone saying "Can you see my screen?"

A person stretching

Someone Yawning

Someone saying, "Sorry I was on mute"

Free Space

Here's a sample card:

| Can you hear me? | Can you see my screen? | I can't see your screen | Dog barking | Two people talk at once |
|---|---|---|---|---|
| I need to take a quick break | Can you hear me? | Someone takes a sip of drink | Sorry, I was on mute | Hello? |
| Someone gets distracted | Your screen froze | FREE SPACE | Phone rings | Can you see me? |
| Sorry, go ahead. | Someone's at the door | I can't hear you | You're on mute | This is my family |
| We can't see you | Children in the background | You've gone silent | Can you all mute unless you're talking? | You're breaking up |

Instruct the group when the game starts from and that they should shout out Bingo when their card is complete. You may like to add in the first horizontal line and first vertical line as mini prizes. You decide if they have to include the centre square or not.

For variation, you may have a card around the key messages of the session to ensure they are listening.

Copyright © www.trainingsupportteam.com with www.learningplanetonline.com

### DE-BRIEF AND REVIEW:

- You can have some fun with the debrief by asking who they observed for what.
- Ask questions around observation techniques. What were we really paying attention to?
- Be careful to ensure the key messages are being taken in also.

# CONSIDER THE CONSEQUENCES

## OBJECTIVE:

A good activity to demonstrate how much of our stress we create ourselves.

| MATERIAL REQUIRED: | TIME REQUIRED: |
|---|---|
| None | 10 - 15 minutes |

## INSTRUCTIONS:

One interesting thing about stress is that in 90% of cases there isn't anything to actually stress you about but the very thought gives you stress. And it's all in our own mind.

For example: *"I have not yet presented my findings to the whole team and I know they are going to pick holes in it and me."*

Here is an activity that helps to understand that:

1. Ask participants to think about something that makes them stressed
2. Ask them to close their eyes and think through various consequences and reactions that might take place
3. They keep thinking about the same thing for approximately 3 minutes
4. Give them directions to intensify the thought like "What would make it even worse?"
5. All of a sudden say – Stop thinking and open your eyes!
6. Ask them how they feel?
7. Ask "Have any of the consequences happened?"
8. Explain that stress in most cases is just your own mental picture and you make it worse by thinking through everything that can go wrong.

## DE-BRIEF AND REVIEW:

### ASK THE GROUP:

- How can we use to reduce our stress levels?
- How can we apply this at work?

# CUTE BABY

### OBJECTIVE:

To help the team members get to know each other a little better. It's a bit of fun and requires a little bit of prep time.

| MATERIAL REQUIRED: | TIME REQUIRED: |
|---|---|
| Baby photos of each team member | 15 minutes |

### INSTRUCTIONS:

Ask each team member to send you a picture of them as a baby. Explain that these pictures will be shared with the rest of the team for this exercise.

During the session, show each picture to the group with a number on the picture. Ask the group to note who they think it is. Wait until all pictures have been shown and do a reveal. Ask the group to mark their own scores. You could ask the group to shout out on the count of 3 as to who they think the person is.

A variation is that you could send the photos round to the group and ask them to note who they think the pictures are of and send them in to you and reveal a winner that way.

### DE-BRIEF AND REVIEW:

**ASK THE GROUP:**

- Were there surprises?
- Who has changed the most?

# DESERT ISLAND

### OBJECTIVE:

This activity helps the group to learn about prioritising and to be open to new ideas and open minds based on new information.

| MATERIAL REQUIRED: | TIME REQUIRED: |
|---|---|
| A list of survival gear and a pen and paper per person | 15 – 25 minutes |

### INSTRUCTIONS:

Explain to the group that each person has been stranded on a desert island. There are a few items floating in the water that they can grab but they will only be able to carry three of them before the rest are washed away.

Give them a list of items they can choose from and ask them to take 3 to 5 minutes to choose their top three. Here is a sample list. You can add more items – don't worry about the survival aspects of each item – just give them a list – they will be the ones thinking creatively:

- A knife
- A box of matches
- A first aid kit
- A sheet of canvas
- A mirror
- 1 KG of chocolate
- A compass
- A lighter
- Ice skates
- Fishing line
- 1 litre of rum
- A hat

After giving them 3 to 5 minutes to choose their items, have each person share what they chose and why. Allow the others in the group to ask questions if they feel they want to. After everyone has shared, give everyone another 3 to 5 minutes to decide if they want to change their minds about any of the items.

Have the group reconvene and share any changes they made and why.

### DE-BRIEF AND REVIEW:

Discuss the principle that we can be open to change when we have new information.

**ASK THE GROUP:**

- Was anyone totally closed to change even though there may have been a better alternative?
- What prevents us from changing?
- What else can we learn from this activity?

# DICE EXERCISE

### OBJECTIVE:

This sales training game aims to demonstrate the point that sales is a numbers game.

| MATERIAL REQUIRED: | TIME REQUIRED: |
|---|---|
| Dice | 10 – 15 minutes depending on size of the group. |

### INSTRUCTIONS:

It's a simple activity which only requires dice. The dice activity involves asking for participants to throw as many of one chosen number as they can within a specified period (recommend 30 seconds per person).

Give each person a turn and if possible, point their camera / screen at the table so everyone else can see the results of the throws.

Set a timer and tell the participant when they have a few seconds left to roll the dice.

This activity is to demonstrate the point that sales is a numbers game and the more you participate (more times you roll the dice) the higher the chance of getting your chosen number (close a sale).

### DE-BRIEF AND REVIEW:

**ASK THE GROUP:**

- Discuss with the team how numbers are important in sales and if you double or triple the number calls or visits or proposals you stand a higher chance of getting your goal. Ask the group:
- Did you notice how people changed their speed of rolling the dice the more under pressure they got?
- Would we stand a higher chance of getting our goals if we focused on the same correct prospects instead of choosing a different number before throw (each visit or phone call)?

# DUCKS IN A ROW

### OBJECTIVE:

This activity enables participants to devise a step by step decision-making process they can use when challenging leadership situations occur.

| MATERIAL REQUIRED: | TIME REQUIRED: |
| --- | --- |
| Paper and pen for each person | 10 - 30 minutes |

### INSTRUCTIONS:

Ask participants to form pairs (use break out rooms in your conference software or have them phone each other and discuss). Then, ask them to come up with the steps that an effective leader goes through in order to work out how to manage a difficult situation.

You can talk about different difficult situations as examples but the steps should be able to apply to any difficult situation - for example:

- Employee is consistently late
- Two staff members arguing
- Change coming but not sure what the details are

After about 15 minutes, bring everyone back together and ask each pair to review the steps they have come up with for the group, and to discuss any thoughts that come out.

After all the pairs have done their reviews have a group discussion about the three to five most effective steps to take in a difficult leadership situation.

### DE-BRIEF AND REVIEW:

**ASK THE GROUP:**

- Who will use these steps next time you face a challenging situation?
- What have you learnt from hearing the different processes?

# EMPLOYEE SPOTLIGHT

### OBJECTIVE:

To help remote teams learn something about each other and have some fun

| MATERIAL REQUIRED: | TIME REQUIRED: |
|---|---|
| None | 5 - 10 minutes |

### INSTRUCTIONS:

Every meeting can feature one of your co-workers before the normal meeting commences. It's optional whether to give advanced notice to the person or choose someone at random at the start of the meeting.

Give the selected person a short amount of time to introduce themselves however they would like. They can share pictures of their family; present a song they have written or what have you. Screen-sharing makes this feasible for remote meetings as well. Hosts can grant screen sharing access to the person of honour to use as they please.

### DE-BRIEF AND REVIEW:

Keep the group on track and focussed on learning something new about a member of the team

**ASK THE GROUP:**

- What did we learn about each other?
- What other variations could we do?

# EXCUSES, EXCUSES

### OBJECTIVE:

This remote energizer is a bit of fun and also helps the group to work on creative skills. It can also be a useful activity for problem solving workshops.

| MATERIAL REQUIRED: | TIME REQUIRED: |
|---|---|
| Paper and pen for each person | 5 - 10 minutes |

### INSTRUCTIONS:

Provide a list of situations where people will need to provide an excuse such as the following:

- Forgot anniversary
- Didn't do homework
- Assignment is not finished
- Being late to work
- Can't go out
- Didn't get the project done

Ask the group to individually come up with the craziest excuses they can for these situations. Give them a few minutes then share them with the wider group.

### DE-BRIEF AND REVIEW:

**ASK THEM:**

- How did you come up with the excuses?
- Did you have personal experience?
- Did ideas grow from other ideas?
- Did you have so many you had to choose which ones you liked best?
- How could we apply this activity to our roles?

# FAVOURITES

### OBJECTIVE:

This is an icebreaker activity that can be applied to product knowledge, sales, stress or any other topic.

| MATERIAL REQUIRED: | TIME REQUIRED: |
|---|---|
| Prepared list or set of images | 15 – 25 minutes |

### INSTRUCTIONS:

Prepare a list of items or images. These can be sent out to the group at the start of a day or the day before if you'd like to give the time some time to consider or you could do it on the spot.

Share an item or show an image and ask each person in turn to share their favourite version of that item. Start with some simple things like: Favourite ice cream or Favourite make of car.

The you can move on to things related to the topic in hand:

- Favourite stress management technique
- Favourite product or service we offer
- Favourite value of the business
- Favourite customer etc

Have each person share their favourite so each person gets a turn.

To make this more meaningful, you could ask the group to share their reasons why they chose that favourite, This could open up better discussion and understanding. This is particularly useful for sales, product knowledge, managing stress etc

### DE-BRIEF AND REVIEW:

**ASK THE GROUP:**
- What did we learn?
- What else could we include?

# FIRST IMPRESSIONS

### OBJECTIVE:

To help the group see how strong and important other people's first impressions of them and others can be. A good energizer for a session starter.

| MATERIAL REQUIRED: | TIME REQUIRED: |
| --- | --- |
| Images pre-prepared | 10 - 20 minutes |

### INSTRUCTIONS:

Have a few images prepared of people. Try to make them people that the group won't recognise, so avoid celebrities. Pictures from magazines or random websites can work for this.

Have the group share their first impressions based solely on what they see in the picture. Get them to describe why they share their impressions like "This man looks like a CEO – his head is held up high and he's wearing an expensive suit."

Allow other group members to agree or disagree but give reasons based on what they see.

Repeat with other images.

### DE-BRIEF AND REVIEW:

Explain that first impressions happen whether they are fair or not – they do exist.

Ask:

- Was it easy to agree on a first impression?
- Why did we have disagreements? What can cause them?
- What are some judgments people are making about us
- Does this have implications for us in our roles?

# GENERIC SALES

### OBJECTIVE:

A good way to test knowledge of products and closing skills of your team.

| MATERIAL REQUIRED: | TIME REQUIRED: |
|---|---|
| Selection of cards or paper with one letter A-Z on each piece | 10 – 30 minutes depending on size of the group. |

### INSTRUCTIONS:

To increase your sales team's abilities. Sometimes selecting random generic products can be harder than selling your known products.

Tell the team they are going to take it in turns (randomly selecting people) and you will flip through the cards / paper without them seeing the letters and they shout stop. The letter that is stopped on is shown and the rest of the team can select any random product or service starting with that letter.

The person whose turn it is then has to do a convincing pitch to the rest of the group and try to 'sell' them the product. The round is over when the team or you decide they have done a good job.

This can be varied to only choosing your own in-house items based on the letter selected or pre making hilarious items (New leather boots for King Kong) on cards and choosing random cards.

### DE-BRIEF AND REVIEW:

Discuss how hard it was coming up with sales skills on a random product on the spot and what they can do to constantly increase their skills.

# GET DRESSED

### OBJECTIVE:

To learn more about each other and have a bit of fun at the same time. A good energizer to use at the start of a session.

| **MATERIAL REQUIRED:** | **TIME REQUIRED:** |
|---|---|
| Extra clothes to have ready | 10 - 20 minutes |

### INSTRUCTIONS:

In advance, ask the group to prepare some extra clothes for this activity. Agree on a number of items to use – at least five items but you could do more. Suggestions for five items could be:

Hat, scarf, gloves x 2 and a jacket

Prepare a set of fun things people may have done or know how to do as your set of questions and read them out one by one. If someone has done or can do what is asked, they put on a piece of clothing. You may have an order to follow if the items are the same for everyone.

Example questions:

- Who has been to Africa?
- Who can play the piano?
- Who has more than three siblings?
- Who is the oldest child in their family?

You can get the group to come up with questions to help too and then randomise the order of questions. You could do several rounds or even reverse the game by being dressed and taking off the 5 extra items.

### DE-BRIEF AND REVIEW:

**ASK THE GROUP:**

- Who learnt something new?
- Do you feel more connected as a group?
- Has this spurred you on to do anything from the questions asked?

# GUESS WHO

### OBJECTIVE:

To break the ice at the start of a group session when participants already know each other. A way of building a team and getting to know each other better.

| MATERIAL REQUIRED: | TIME REQUIRED: |
|---|---|
| Pre work – sending out information and getting it back beforehand | 15 minutes dependent upon the number of participants |

### INSTRUCTIONS:

Send out a short questionnaire and get the team to send it back before the session. Explain that these answers will be revealed at an upcoming session. Examples of questions to include:

- Favourite film?
- Favourite television programme?
- Favourite food?
- Favourite music?
- Pet hate?
- Famous person you admire?
- Your ideal holiday?
- A unique fact about yourself

Select each person's response sheet at random and read out the answers given. Ask the groups to guess who is who.

### DE-BRIEF AND REVIEW:

**ASK THEM:**

- What did you learn during this activity?
- What surprised you?

# HACKATHON

## OBJECTIVE:

This is an opportunity for you and your team to come up with new ideas and improvements on existing processes and products or services.

| MATERIAL REQUIRED: | TIME REQUIRED: |
|---|---|
| None | 20 - 30 minutes |

## INSTRUCTIONS:

The idea for this activity is to pick a focus area and run some rounds on questioning what you do. For example, you can pick a process like: Customer purchasing or Approving new purchases. As a group, as a question like: "What is one thing you would change about this process?"

Allow the group to answer and share their reasons. Look for concurrence from others and table any suggestions that are obvious, common or worth looking at for further discussion. You don't need to go deep in this meeting. This meeting is for idea generating.

Another option is to take a product or service you have and ask: "What's one thing you would change about this product?"

Again, allow the group to share thoughts and ideas. Table those for a later discussion you think could be useful.

Ensure you say at the beginning that you are not looking to finalise anything just yet – this meeting is for generating ideas only, that way you won't disappoint those who felt you should have gone further.

## DE-BRIEF AND REVIEW:

Continuous improvement is all about challenging the norm and the status quo. That's how improvements are made. Encourage this type of thinking.

**ASK THE GROUP:**

- What improvements have you noticed about products you use over the years?
- What else should we look at?

# HAPPY HOUR

### OBJECTIVE:

A fun way to end the week and have the team interact in a relaxed way.

| **MATERIAL REQUIRED:** | **TIME REQUIRED:** |
|---|---|
| None | No set time |

### INSTRUCTIONS:

Organise a virtual happy hour at the end of the week (usually a Friday afternoon around 4.30 – 5pm). A fun time where everyone can drink and be themselves. Non-drinkers can bring along a soda or water — it's less about the drink and more about the happy hour chatting and getting to know each other and discussing the week or projects etc.

Every member of the team is encouraged to join in even people who had never gone to a normal happy hour with the team! People need contact with others and this can be one of the best professional icebreakers for people who might not want to be out and about in these types of extravert situations.

### DE-BRIEF AND REVIEW:

- A fun way to help break the ice and help the teams get to know each other better in a less formal setting. You could ask the group:
- What did we learn?
- How are we feeling?

# HASHTAG DAY

### OBJECTIVE:

To help the group share how they're feeling about the day, the week or any particular topic. Could be used at the start of a session, end of the day etc.

| MATERIAL REQUIRED: | TIME REQUIRED: |
|---|---|
| None | 10 – 15 minutes |

### INSTRUCTIONS:

Explain to the group that they will have 30 seconds to share how their day has gone by:

1. Using a hashtag and
2. Sharing a song title that aptly sums it up

For Example:

1. #Headsinaspin or #manic
2. "Dizzy" by Vic Reeves and the Wonderstuff

Have each person share in turn. A little explanation could be shared too.

Variations on this could be:

- Start of the shift reflecting on yesterday
- About the new changes in the business
- About a specific product
- About a recent sales experience
- About a specific customer

### DE-BRIEF AND REVIEW:

**ASK THE GROUP:**

Have the group comment on the general feel.

- What can we glean from the explanations?
- Were there similarities?
- How do we feel now?
- Do we need to change anything?

# HEADACHE

## OBJECTIVE:

To illustrate what type of questions we need to use to gain information, the different responses we receive when using different questions and the importance of listening to the customers' responses. This activity also shows how long a situation can go on for when a scattered approach is used for questioning versus a structured approach.

| **MATERIAL REQUIRED:** | **TIME REQUIRED:** |
|---|---|
| None | 10 - 15 minutes |

## INSTRUCTIONS:

Explain to the group that that we are going to have a quiz. Explain that they are doctors and their task is to diagnose what is causing my headaches and how to avoid them for the future. DO NOT go down the medical route as they don't know enough and also it is not medically related.

Rules of the game: Each person gets a chance to ask one question at a time, If you ask more than one question I will only answer one of them; if you cannot think of a question you can pass

You have 3 minutes planning time to list all the questions you want to ask.

At this point discreetly get a piece of paper and draw up a page to record number of open questions and closed questions (It is important that the group do not know what you are recording at this stage)

Only respond to the type of question the group has asked i.e. if they ask a closed question respond with a yes or no – if they ask an open question, answer with that detail required – do not give extra information

When you start the activity, before they plan the questions – begin with: "I have a headache and I would like you tell me how to avoid it happening in the future" - let them plan then you can start by repeating the question and alternate between the people in the group, recording open and closed questions on your sheet of paper.

Other Details you need to know and provide – only if the question is asked:

- Had headaches for the last 3 months
- Get them on a Sunday afternoon and they go by Monday mid-morning
- Your job is a corporate trainer
- You started new hobbies about 3 months ago which are (make some up such as oil painting, motor mechanics, photography AND community work). They will think elements in the hobbies are giving headaches such oils or chemicals in photo's etc. Must include the community work.

- You help out and go to church every Sunday morning – Only say this when you are asked directly what your community service is OR what you do on a Sunday morning
- You help out at church by ringing the bell – Do NOT tell them this one unless asked what you do at church!
- What will happen:
- Due to the time constraints they will not be able to list all of the questions they need to ask to find the answers. When they run out of questions they will AUTOMATICALLY switch to closed questions (every group does!).
- They will give you a scattered approach to the questions
- They may compete with the other team by not following from each other's questions
- They may not listen to the other people and therefore ask the same questions others have asked

They may begin to get frustrated when they cannot seem to find answers (at this point stop them and review the facts for them)

## DE-BRIEF AND REVIEW:

- Explain to the group the need to have a plan of all the critical information they need and then format the questions to obtain this information in a timely and structured manner
- Explain what happens if we jump to conclusions – we get the wrong answer or can confuse the customer, longer call times etc.
- As you progress through the activity people will jump in and TELL you what's wrong before they know!!!
- Share the category headings and ask what categories we could have listed our questions under.
-     Timeframe        Health        Hobbies        Changes        Work
- How different do you think the activity would be if we had asked our questions like this as opposed to the shotgun / scattered approach??

# HEADS AND TAILS

### OBJECTIVE:

This quick energizer can be used to get people up and on their feet and engaged to start a session.

| MATERIAL REQUIRED: | TIME REQUIRED: |
|---|---|
| Two coins | 5 minutes |

### INSTRUCTIONS:

Ask the group to stand up and adjust their camera to suit so they can all be seen. Explain that you will be tossing two coins in the air and calling out if they landed as heads or tails or one of each.

The group, before the coins are tossed must decide individually what they predict the coins will land as. If they believe both will be heads, they place two hands on their head. If they believe both will land as tails, they place both hands on their bottoms. If they believe one coin will be head and one tails, they place one hand on their head and one on their bottom.

Ensure everyone has made their choice, and then toss the coins.

Anyone who guesses right continues to stand for the next round. Anyone that got it wrong is eliminated.

Continue until one person is left standing. If the last people are eliminated together, replay that round.

Variations can include using dice and calling odds and evens.

Consider a prize for the winner after several complete rounds or each complete round.

### DE-BRIEF AND REVIEW:

You could ask how the group are feeling. They should be energized and ready to go.

# HELP FROM MY COLLEAGUES

### OBJECTIVE:

A team activity to help everyone understand what the team needs when they are stressed.

| MATERIAL REQUIRED: | TIME REQUIRED: |
|---|---|
| Paper and pen for each person | 10 - 15 minutes |

### INSTRUCTIONS:

Get everyone to write their name at the top of a piece of paper. Then add the following: -

1. What I need my colleagues to do when I'm stressed is …. (fill in the blank)
2. What I need my colleagues NOT to do when I'm stressed is … (fill in the blank)

Take a few minutes to share this information with each other as a team. The information is copied and emailed in to the organiser then collated, and every member of the team is given a copy for future reference.

The understanding that occurs through discussion is amazing because people recognise very quickly that we all have different needs and should never assume that what you need/don't need is the same as for others.

### DE-BRIEF AND REVIEW:

**ASK THE GROUP:**

- Who learnt something new?
- Were there similarities?
- Is anyone planning to adopt a change as a result?

# I WOULD BE...

### OBJECTIVE:

This activity can be used as an icebreaker or as an activity to break up a session. It will help the team to get to know each other a bit better too.

| MATERIAL REQUIRED: | TIME REQUIRED: |
|---|---|
| None | 10 - 20 minutes |

### INSTRUCTIONS:

As children, we all had dream jobs we wanted to do. Even now, we may still have a fond dream of what we would do if we didn't need to earn money.

In turn, ask each person to share what they would be if they weren't doing what they currently are doing. This could be a job that they would prefer to do if money didn't count or opportunities were there. These things may include being a famous sports star, a singer, an astronaut etc.

Normally these things are out of reach but fun to think about.

Linking what people like about those things to their current role could be quite powerful. For example, a person that works in a contact centre that would rather be opera singing may struggle to find a link. But asking the question, "What is it you like about Opera singing?' may provide some clues. For example, if they like the way it makes people feel when they sing opera – then they can link that back to their role and help people feel good when they talk to them on the phone. The link is helping people feel good.

### DE-BRIEF AND REVIEW:

**ASK THE GROUP:**

- Why would you want to do those things?
- Is there something about those things that you like that you could relate or link to your current role?
- What is it you like best about your current role?

# INTRODUCTION BY ASSOCIATION

### OBJECTIVE:

To help break the ice at the beginning of a virtual session and get to know each other.

| MATERIAL REQUIRED: | TIME REQUIRED: |
|---|---|
| None | 5 minutes |

### INSTRUCTIONS:

Explain that this exercise is to help learning by the use of association.

Remind the group that it could be used in a work context if they are having difficulty in remembering something.

Tell the group that they are to introduce themselves to the group by stating their first given name and associating their name with something they would bring to a picnic.

For example: My name is Fred, and I'd bring some bread.

Possible Variation:

Tell the group they will be asked to introduce themselves to the group by stating their first given name and associating their name with a personal characteristic that helps identify them, and to do so in the form of a rhyme.

For example: My name is Sue, with eyes of blue.

### DE-BRIEF AND REVIEW:

**ASK THEM:**
- Who found that hard?
- What did they learn?
- How could we apply this to our workplace?

# INTRODUCTION QUESTIONS

### OBJECTIVE:

An interesting way for team members to get to know one another or a new person joining the team.

| MATERIAL REQUIRED: | TIME REQUIRED: |
|---|---|
| None | 10 - 15 minutes |

### INSTRUCTIONS:

The best way to get to know someone is to ask them questions. Having new team members ask the questions makes it so they are learning exactly what they are interested in.

Everyone in the meeting can start with the same simple questions, such as their name and age, and then the floor can be opened to questions from the rest of the group. The information you will learn about each person will be unique and more easily remembered.

Most video-calling technology enables you to highlight individual participants, so you can always focus on who is being introduced. In apps such as Zoom, questions can be submitted via chatbox or through the "raise hand" feature to ensure that interruptions are held to a minimum.

### DE-BRIEF AND REVIEW:

- This activity should give you some really insights into people by the types of questions they are asking.
- If you have a new person listen for what questions the existing team are asking and look at how you can build this information into an introduction for new people moving forward.

# LAUGHTER IS THE BEST MEDICINE

### OBJECTIVE:

A great opportunity to have a good laugh as a team and show how it reduces stress.

| MATERIAL REQUIRED: | TIME REQUIRED: |
| --- | --- |
| Something each person finds funny | 10 - 15 minutes |

### INSTRUCTIONS:

Laughter causes the brain to produce dopamine, the chemical responsible for feelings of happiness. By improving your mood, laughter allows you to gain a different perspective on difficult situations and connect more easily with others. Laughing as a group relieves stress and can form stronger bonds within the group.

**MATERIALS**

Each of your team will need the following:

Anything that can make them laugh:

- Videos, Comics, Cards, Memes, Photos, Jokes, Stories

Have each person share their item with the group.

Allow the group to benefit from each member's laughter.

**ALTERNATE METHODS**

You can try these alternate methods, as well.

- Find a funny video or movie to watch as a group.
- Have everyone tell a story regarding:
- An embarrassing moment
- The funniest thing they can remember happening to them
- Have a place that everyone can write down funny moments and send in and come together in a group to share them.

### DE-BRIEF AND REVIEW:

**ASK THE GROUP:**

- Who feels less stressed?

# LEADERS YOU ADMIRE

### OBJECTIVE:

A good activity for personal reflection and development of skill traits.

| MATERIAL REQUIRED: | TIME REQUIRED: |
| --- | --- |
| None | 10 - 30 minutes |

### INSTRUCTIONS:

This activity involves participants being divided into groups or pairs. If your online conference system has break out rooms then this is great otherwise have people call each other to discuss.

The pairs or groups (you can run this as one large group if there aren't too many in the group) are to choose and discuss leaders they know or know of (alive, dead or fictional) and why they admire them. They should list the attributes or characteristics that they admire.

Groups come back together for a larger discussion and communication session at the end. This really helps define desirable leadership characteristics and can give the teams areas of personal development to strive towards.

### DE-BRIEF AND REVIEW:

**ASK THE GROUP:**

- Who was surprised at some of the choices and why?
- What personal development as leaders can we take from this?

# LEADERSHIP REFLECTIONS

### OBJECTIVE:

A great activity for exploring different leadership styles.

| **MATERIAL REQUIRED:** | **TIME REQUIRED:** |
|---|---|
| Paper and pen for each person | 10 - 30 minutes |

### INSTRUCTIONS:

We will look at three different 'leadership styles: Autocratic, Delegative and Democratic.

An autocratic leader makes decisions without first consulting others, while a delegative leader allows the staff to make the decisions and a democratic leader consults with the staff in making workplace decisions

The group should be divided into small groups (use breakout rooms in your conference call software or they call each other). Provide participants with the statement 'consider a time when you, or another leader, used the autocratic, democratic or delegative style of leadership'.

Ask participants to reflect on the statement and make a few comments, such as: Was it effective? Would a different leadership style have worked better? What were the experiences? Which style is easiest for them to use and why?

Come together as a whole group and discuss what was learned about the three styles of leadership.

### DE-BRIEF AND REVIEW:

**ASK THE GROUP:**

- Who learnt something new?
- Does it show that different scenarios require different styles?
- How can we learn to adapt our leadership styles?

# LISTENING EXERCISE

### OBJECTIVE:

To demonstrate peoples listening skills and how easily they are distracted either by outside influences or by their own thoughts. Also, what the important things to listen are.

| **MATERIAL REQUIRED:** | **TIME REQUIRED:** |
|---|---|
| Paper and pen for each person | 10 minutes |

### INSTRUCTIONS:

Tell everyone they will have to write EXACTLY what you read out – BUT they cannot begin writing until you have FINISHED reading out each phrase and you tell them begin.

Check everyone has working pen and clean sheet of paper. They are to number each phrase 1 – 5.

Read the following phrases clearly and concisely but only read them out ONCE!! Ensure no-one starts writing until you have finished reading each one out. Get them to write out each phrase after you have read it (not all five at once). Check everyone is finished the current one before you move on.

Read out the following phrases:

1. Gerry said there were 28 pencils and 30 red pens in the blue truck
2. Please tell Martin to add two thousand and 42 dollars and 29 cents to Jim's expense account on Monday the 23rd
3. Ask Bill to bring 24 application forms and 76 pens to the introductory meeting tonight
4. After you have cleaned the bathroom please take care to put the broom back into the closet and the bucket back under the sink
5. When I say you there is no I, and when I say I there is no you

Now check the answers. They must be EXACTLY the same as you read out!

What will happen:

People will struggle to get the answer EXACTLY right as they will forget details, hear different things or get distracted and miss words.

### DE-BRIEF AND REVIEW:

"That was easy wasn't it?"

They will give you responses along the lines of NO etc!!!

Explain that the same thing happens when we are speaking with customers, which is why we must ensure we WRITE notes as we go, we must be engaged and we must paraphrase to ensure we get it right.

**ASK THEM:**

- What plan did you have for trying to remember each phrase?
- Were some more difficult than others?
- What were the important words to remember for each phrase?

Focus on the fact that the numbers, names and colours were more important than some of the other words and yet these were the ones we may have got wrong.

Ask how they can apply this to their roles.

# LISTENING QUIZ

### OBJECTIVE:

This activity demonstrates how we listen through preconceived ideas. We take information we already know and automatically and often apply it to a situation which looks in this case sounds familiar. THIS IS FOR FUN only and should not be taken too seriously.

| **MATERIAL REQUIRED:** | **TIME REQUIRED:** |
|---|---|
| Paper and pen for each person | 10 minutes |

### INSTRUCTIONS:

Explain to the group that you will be running a listening quiz. This is an individual quiz and if you know the answers please do not call them out

"On the left hand side of the page write down 1 to 8"

Wait…

Ask if any participants have written 128 and how many have written 1234….8. Note the instruction and how easy it is to get communication wrong!

Get everyone to write in full 1-8 down the page. Explain you will only read out the questions once and you will not repeat them. Any questions before I start?

Number 1

A man builds a square house and all sides face south, a bear comes to the door and rings the doorbell. What colour is the bear?

Number 2

You walk into a COLD DARK room and in the COLD DARK room you see a candle, a kerosene lamp, an oil heater, and fire place with paper and kindling. (say this bit quickly) You have one match in your matchbox, which do you light FIRST, for maximum HEAT?

Number 3

(say this first part quite quickly) You are the driver of a bus. (Now normally) You leave the bus terminal at EXACTLY 6.57am, at the first stop you pick up 3 men, 3 women and 4 children. At the second stop you pick up 2 children, drop off the women and pick 1 more man. At the third stop you pick up 2 women drop off 2 children and 2 men. At the fourth stop you drop off all the men, pick 3 women and 2 more children.

This goes on all morning until you get back to the bus terminal at EXACTLY 11.57am.

(Pause)

What colour is the bus drivers eyes?

Number 4

According to INTERNATIONAL law when a plane is travelling from one country to another and it crashes on the EXACT border between the countries, according to INTERNATIONAL law where are the survivors buried, in the country they are coming from or the country they are going to, according to INTERNATIONAL law?

Number 5

It's been raining for forty days and forty nights, the rains and floods have come. GOD tells a man to build a large wooden boat and save as many pairs of the animals as he can.

How many pairs of animals did Moses take on board the Ark during the great flood?

Number 6

Can a man marry his widow's sister – yes or No?

Number 7

Do they have a fourth of July in England?

Number 8

Can a man living in Australia be buried in New Zealand?

Number 9 (yes, you said 1-8 – how many were listening? 9 is a bonus)

There are 3 apples and you take away 2 how many do you have?

## DE-BRIEF AND REVIEW:

### ASK THE GROUP:

The aim is to show how quickly we can become confused, misdirected or just switch off when it gets too hard to listen. Go back through the quiz and show where the misdirection took place and why (some people may need to be given the answers again as it may take a while to click!)

Answers are:

- White – it's a Polar Bear (Only place you can build a house with 4 sides facing South is the North Pole)
- The MATCH!!!
- Whatever your eyes are – opening sentence YOU are the driver of a bus!
- We don't bury survivors….
- It wasn't Moses, it was Noah (people hear the opening and jump to conclusions)
- NO – if she is a widow then he is DEAD
- YES of course they do; after the 3rd and before the 5th!!
- No, Because he is LIVING….
- 2 BECAUSE you took of them

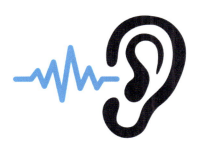

# LOOSE MEANINGS

### OBJECTIVE:

To show that we need to be more specific in our communication – especially if the words or phrases are ambiguous or open to interpretation.

| MATERIAL REQUIRED: | TIME REQUIRED: |
|---|---|
| Paper and pen for each person | 10 minutes |

### INSTRUCTIONS:

Explain to the group that you will read out a number of statements and they are to write down what they think each statement means to them. They are to put timings and pinpoint more information to make it clear:

1. I'll get back to you in a bit
2. I'll load that into the system soon
3. Can I come back to you shortly?
4. You can only do that a few times
5. Lots of people have the same problem
6. It's only a minor thing

At the end of all 6, have the group take turns going round for each point to explain what the statement meant to them. You should get varying responses for each point – eg: "a bit" may mean 1 hour, by the end of the day, within a week etc.

You could get everyone to share their responses by the chat feature of your video conferencing tool. This is a fun way to have everyone see the responses live.

### DE-BRIEF AND REVIEW:

Discuss as a group how we can be more specific for these statements and what it will avoid (assumptions, frustrations etc).

- End with saying there are many more phrases we use that mean different things to different people such as "In a timely manner".

Encourage the group to pick one or two of these phrases and identify what they will do to make more specific and clarified communication as a result.

# MAD HATTER DAYS

### OBJECTIVE:

To have a bit of fun on a conference call and help energise and motivate a team

| MATERIAL REQUIRED: | TIME REQUIRED: |
| --- | --- |
| Hats | Duration of the call |

### INSTRUCTIONS:

Give the team notice that you will be calling for a Mad Hatter Day. This where they have to find or make the most outrageous hat that they can.

They then have to wear their hat for the entire duration of the call.

When the call starts give everyone a few minutes to have a good laugh and discussion around their hats and why they chose what they did and if appropriate select a winner!

### DE-BRIEF AND REVIEW:

- You can have some fun with the debrief by asking who they thought had the most outrageous or who had put the most work / effort in?
- Ask if they had fun and felt like a team and ask for suggestions for the next team fun activity.

# MEMORY TEST

## OBJECTIVE:

To help participants discover basic psychological facts about our memory. It's a fun activity that can be used for any number of people.

| MATERIAL REQUIRED: | TIME REQUIRED: |
|---|---|
| Paper and pen for each person | 10 – 15 minutes |

## INSTRUCTIONS:

Tell them that you are going to administer a memory test. You will read a standardized list of words. Participants should listen carefully to these words without writing them down. Later, you will test to see how many words each participant can recall.

Present words. Read the following list of words. Pause briefly between one word and the next. Do not change the sequence. One of the words (night) is repeated three times:

| Dream | sleep | night | mattress | snooze | Sheet |
|---|---|---|---|---|---|
| nod | tired | night | artichoke | insomnia | blanket |
| night | alarm | nap | snore | pillow | |

Administer the recall test. Pause for about 10 seconds. Ask each participant to take a piece of paper and write as many of the words as he or she can remember. Pause for about 40 seconds.

Explain your intent. Reassure participants that you are not interested in finding out how each person performed on the test. Instead, you are going to use the test to explore four basic principles about memory.

## DE-BRIEF AND REVIEW:

- Here are four important principles about memory. Explain each of them, using data from participants' performance on the test:
- Ask participants to raise their hands if they recalled the words "dream" and "pillow". Explain that people remember the first and the last things in a series. Most participants will have written dream and pillow because they were the first and last words in the list. This is called Primacy and Recency effects.
- Ask participants to raise their hands if they recalled the word "artichoke". Explain that people remember things that are novel or different. Most participants will have written artichoke because it is different from the other words in the list. This is called Surprise effect.
- Ask participants to raise their hands if they recalled the word "night". Explain that people remember things that are repeated. Most participants will have written night because you repeated it three times. This is called Repetition effect.
- Ask participants to raise their hands if they recalled the word "bed". Reveal that this word was not on your list. Explain that the brain closes logical gaps in what it hears, sees, or reads, frequently remembering things that did not take place. Most participants will have written bed because it logically belongs to this list (even though you never read it). This is called False-memory effect.
- Encourage action planning. Ask participants how they would use these four principles to help them remember new terms and ideas in the training session. Give examples such as, "To compensate for the primacy and the recency effects, pay particular attention to ideas presented during the middle of the training session. Make use of the repetition effect by repeating these ideas to yourself several times."

# METAPHORIC GADGETS

### OBJECTIVE:

To help remote teams learn something about each other and have some fun. Also a way to get people to think quickly on their feet, be creative and learn that having something concrete in front of you helps.

| **MATERIAL REQUIRED:** | **TIME REQUIRED:** |
|---|---|
| None | 10 - 15 minutes |

### INSTRUCTIONS:

Ask each person to take one minute and go and find an object from a particular place that represents something relevant to the topic.

For example, "You all have one minute to go and bring back an object from the kitchen that represents what value you bring to the team".

When everyone is back, get them to show what their object is and what it represents. Allow everyone the same time to share.

You could repeat with another topic and new rules as to where to go. For example, "You have one minute to go and bring back an object from the bathroom that represents how you are feeling right now". Again, allow all people to share within a timeframe – suggest 10 - 20 seconds each.

### DE-BRIEF AND REVIEW:

Keep the instructions short and say 'Go!' when you conclude the instructions. Everyone will want to be involved – as no one will want to be the only one without an object. Choose someone who you know gets the idea to go first. You don't have to join in unless you want to..

**ASK THE GROUP:**
- What did we learn about each other?
- Who found it difficult? Why or why not?
- What did you learn about yourself?
- What other variations could we do?

# MULTITASKING MYTH

## OBJECTIVE:

To illustrate what can happen when we try to do more than one thing at once. A good icebreaker or part of a training session around time management and working practices.

| MATERIAL REQUIRED: | TIME REQUIRED: |
|---|---|
| A pen and paper for each participant<br>Stopwatch or watch | 10 – 15 minutes |

## INSTRUCTIONS:

Explain to the group that you will be asking them to write down two lines of information on a piece of paper.

You may want to prepare a slide and share your screen with what you mean. Tell them that when you say 'Go', they are to write the sentence "Multi-tasking disengages the brain" on one line, then write out the full alphabet underneath on the next line as follows:

"Multitasking disengages the brain"

"abcdefghijklmnopqrstuvwxyz"

When they are finished they are to shout out "Complete'. Using a watch or stopwatch record each person's time to completion. 'Go!'

When everyone has finished, tell them we are going to do the exercise again but this time, as they write each letter of the sentence you drop down and write a letter of the alphabet underneath.

E.g. after 'm' on the top line write 'a' below the 'm', After 'u' write 'b' below the 'u, After 'l' write 'c' below the 'i'. After 't' write 'd' below the 't' etc. Show them on a slide what you mean.

Using a watch or stopwatch time each person to completion again. 'Go!'

What will happen:

The first sentence and alphabet will be done quite quickly. People usually do it in approximately 30 seconds. The second attempt is much harder to do.

Some people will give it a go through to the end.

Others will give up in frustration and confusion.

Their writing and accuracy will deteriorate the second time.

### DE-BRIEF AND REVIEW:

**ASK THE GROUP:**
- What was the difference between the two attempts?
- How easy was it to concentrate each time?
- What difference was there in the time taken to complete the two tasks?
- Was there a change in quality?
- Do you habitually multi-task?

Explain that this is what happens when we try to multi-task at work, at home and when driving. Multi-tasking is not effective. We actually move between tasks very quickly even though we seem to be doing them at the same time. Those little moves decrease our effectiveness and we should try to complete a task before moving on to the next.

# MY MOMENT

## OBJECTIVE:

To help the team members get to know each other. This may also uncover some new insights for the business.

| MATERIAL REQUIRED: | TIME REQUIRED: |
| --- | --- |
| None | 5 minutes |

## INSTRUCTIONS:

Schedule some time during a session to focus on one team member and give them their moment.

This team member then has 5 minutes to share some things that could include:

- Where they were born
- Previous Roles
- Siblings and family members
- One thing they would change about the organisation
- Their superpower or talent
- Something people might not know about them etc

Try and keep the same list for each staff member. Allow them to add something else themselves. Do a fresh list when you have done one round. This is designed for one person per session so they feel like they have their moment.

## DE-BRIEF AND REVIEW:

**ASK THE GROUP:**

- What did you learn?
- Do you have questions?

# NEVER DONE THAT

### OBJECTIVE:

This activity allows people to learn a bit more about their co-workers. It's a fun activity to do at the start of a session or ending a shift.

| **MATERIAL REQUIRED:** | **TIME REQUIRED:** |
|---|---|
| None | 10 – 15 minutes |

### INSTRUCTIONS:

Each person holds up one hand with 5 fingers raised. Allow each person in the group to take turns saying one thing they haven't done. Anyone that has done that thing must lower one finger. Those that haven't done that thing leave their fingers up.

For example, if someone says, "I've never been swimming in the ocean" then if someone has been swimming in the ocean, they lower a finger.

Each person in turn says one thing they haven't done and the same rule applies. When a person lowers their last finger, they are eliminated. The person that is the last one with at least one finger raised wins.

You may like to have a few family-friendly things as options if people can't think of anything at all – or you could give some examples.

### DE-BRIEF AND REVIEW:

- This is a fun way to get to know people better in the group. You could ask the group:
- Were there any surprises?
- What thing lowered most fingers?
- What have you learnt about the group as a whole?

# NOT MY JOB

### OBJECTIVE:

To help team members understand certain frustrations that people have. This could be useful for teams or departments that work together or for inter-departmental issues.

| **MATERIAL REQUIRED:** | **TIME REQUIRED:** |
|---|---|
| Paper and pen for each person | 10 minutes |

### INSTRUCTIONS:

Have everyone in the group introduce themselves as part of this exercise. Even teams that know each other, this is a great little exercise to run. As part of the exercise, each person is to tell everyone else their name and role then to add three things that *aren't* part of their job.

Give them a couple of minutes before you start to think up three things and allow them to write them down.

People will often share things that they often do that aren't part of their job which will be good for people to hear.

### DE-BRIEF AND REVIEW:

**ASK THE GROUP:**

- Were there any surprises there?
- What can we utilise from that exercise back in our roles?

# OBJECTION!

## OBJECTIVE:

To help the team come up with ways to handle objections better about the products, services or company. Good sales and customer service activity.

| MATERIAL REQUIRED: | TIME REQUIRED: |
|---|---|
| None | 15 – 30 minutes |

## INSTRUCTIONS:

One at a time, have someone share something positive about a product, service or about the organisation. This should be a statement about it like:

"Our car batteries are cheap and easy to install"

Then ask for suggestions as to what may be classed as an objection or an issue with what was said about the product like:

"They actually don't last very long though and need replacing more than the competitors."

The group then has to come up with a statement or response that will counter that objection like:

"Most of the customers we deal with prefer to have something affordable and as they are so easy to install, replacing one twice is still cheaper and easier than trying to fit a longer lasting more expensive one."

Discuss further until you can agree on a response or group of responses to help handle the objection and pick another product or service or statement about the business.

## DE-BRIEF AND REVIEW:

- Having responses to objections that may be raised in advance gives you confidence in your role. You could talk about experiences people have had in this area. You can also build in the response to your pitch so the objections aren't ever raised.
- Ask if there are any objections people have found too hard to deal with and work on those.

# PAPER FOLDING

### OBJECTIVE:

To illustrate the point that even with the same instructions, people will interpret them differently. Clarification around instructions is vital to ensure people understand exactly what is meant by them.

| MATERIAL REQUIRED: | TIME REQUIRED: |
|---|---|
| Piece of A4 paper for everyone | 10 minutes |

### INSTRUCTIONS:

Ensure everyone has a sheet of paper. Tell everyone to close their eyes and follow your instructions.

Start giving instructions about what to do with the piece of paper examples:

- fold it in half
- fold the lower left corner over the upper right corner
- turn it 90 degrees to the left
- rip a half-circle in the middle of the right side
- Turn the paper upside down
- fold it again
- Tear off an inch from the top of the paper
- …add a couple more instructions if you like

Once you have given the instructions, tell everyone to open their eyes and unfold their piece of paper. Even though they all received the same instructions and had the same starting material, pretty much everyone will have a different result.

### DE-BRIEF AND REVIEW:

Areas to discuss and share with the group:

- We don't all start with the same base (some held their piece of paper vertically or horizontally) so we don't all have the same results
- Some interpreted to rip a piece of paper as removing a big piece, some as a small piece
- Having eyes closed = not receiving feedback on our performance
- Some instructions appear vague to some and clear to others.

# PERSPECTIVE VIEW

### OBJECTIVE:

To help people in the group see things from a different point of view. This activity can be used for any topic or problem solving session.

| MATERIAL REQUIRED: | TIME REQUIRED: |
|---|---|
| Pens and paper. Virtual Breakout rooms | 10 - 20 minutes |

### INSTRUCTIONS:

Have a topic that the group needs to discuss. This could be about a process, a product, a situation or something that the group needs to resolve or brainstorm about. For example: Our complaints process.

Have a list of options available or have the group come up with a list of potential stakeholders or roles that could be involved or affected by the situation chosen. For example:

- The Manager
- A New Customer
- Biggest Competitor
- Biggest Customer
- Potential New Competitor
- Old Employee
- New Employee

Divide the group into smaller groups of 2 or 3, put them into breakout rooms or discuss offline how their stakeholder sees this issue. Give them 5 - 10 minutes and get them to brainstorm thoughts based on the role they have been given from the list. Invite the groups to have more than one shot at this by changing the role so they get more than one perspective. Discuss the perspectives as a wider group.

### DE-BRIEF AND REVIEW:

**ASK THEM:**

- Did the role allow you to see things from a different perspective?
- What new ideas came as a result of having a new role to think from?
- What do we need to do as a result of what we discovered?
- Are there any other roles we could include?

# PHONE PICS

### OBJECTIVE:

To help the group get to know something about each other quickly. To help the group open up a bit more and build trust. Knowing more about a person can help to build more trust.

| **MATERIAL REQUIRED:** | **TIME REQUIRED:** |
|---|---|
| Each person to use their mobile phones | 5 - 10 minutes |

### INSTRUCTIONS:

Have each person open up their photos on their mobile phones. Ask them to choose one or two pictures they will be prepared to share with the rest of the group that they love or that says something about them or that they're proud of.

Ask the group to take turns to share the photos they've chosen with the group. Have the group listen to their story which should include why they selected those particular photos and the story behind them. Give a time frame for each person.

Allow each person to share their chosen photos.

### DE-BRIEF AND REVIEW:

Explain that activities like this don't take long and help to bond the group.

**ASK THE GROUP:**

- Who had fun doing that?
- Were there any surprises?
- Who learnt something?
- How do we feel as a group?

# PLANTS AND ANIMALS

## OBJECTIVE:

To help participants in the group to get to know each other. This exercise is spread over more than the session so it keeps people thinking.

| MATERIAL REQUIRED: | TIME REQUIRED: |
|---|---|
| Paper and pens | 10 - 20 minutes reveal plus some pre-time to allow participants to complete |

## INSTRUCTIONS:

### PRE-TIME:

Ask everyone in the group to think up a name for themselves based on the following:

- Their new first name must be a plant, vegetable, flower or tree
- Their new second name must be an animal, fish or bird

For example: – Hyacinth Rabbit or Daffodil Shark or Rose Eagle

Explain to them that they will need to be able to explain why they have chosen their particular name in a later session but that they must not let the other group participants know what they have chosen yet.

The chosen names should be sent back to you by email. Once you have everyone's name in, distribute them to the whole group and give them some time to consider who is who. Prepare a sheet for each participant to make it easier for them. Give them the day or overnight and specify when we will be revealing the answers.

### REVEAL SESSION TIME:

At the designated session, lead the group in revealing who is who, what their co-workers thought, and why each person chose their particular name. You could share the name and share who thought they were then have the actual person reveal who it really was and why they chose the name.

## DE-BRIEF AND REVIEW:

- This is an opportunity to get to know each other well. Thank them for participating. Ask if anyone would choose different names next time and why.

# POOR CUSTOMER SERVICE

### OBJECTIVE:

To help participants understand both what to say and what not to say in customer service situations. It helps people to be able to rephrase their statements in a positive way.

| **MATERIAL REQUIRED:** | **TIME REQUIRED:** |
|---|---|
| None | 10 – 15 minutes |

### INSTRUCTIONS:

Explain that each person will have an opportunity to rephrase a poor customer service statement and come up with another poor example. Agree some method of order for the group – Alphabetical for example.

The first person in the group is to come up with a phrase that is not right and should not be said to a customer such as:

"You don't know what you're talking about".

The next person in the group order is to then change the wording of the statement in a positive way such as:

"Thank you for sharing your thoughts".

That person then comes up with a negative example of a phrase you should never say to a customer and the next person must rephrase positively.

Other examples:

"You've come through to the wrong place"

"No, that's wrong"

"You don't understand"

"If you'd just listen to me"

Don't allow too much time to think and move on to the next person if they struggle.

### DE-BRIEF AND REVIEW:

**ASK THE GROUP:**

- Which negative phrases have you used in the past? What about the positive ones?
- What do you think the effect of these negative statements could be on customers?
- Which phrase was easier to come up with under pressure – negative or positive?

# POSITIVE RESPONSE

### OBJECTIVE:

To show people they can answer with a positive instead of a negative

| MATERIAL REQUIRED: | TIME REQUIRED: |
|---|---|
| None | 10 – 15 minutes |

### INSTRUCTIONS:

When dealing with customers it is important that we respond positively whenever we can instead of telling them what we can't do.

This activity will get people thinking out the square instead of just saying what they can't do!

Tell the group that they will take it in turns to be asked something they cannot say yes to but instead of just saying no or saying they can't do it they must respond positively. When the round is finished, the person who was being asked gets to choose the next person and then asks then for something.

The rounds continue until everyone has had a turn

**HERE'S AN EXAMPLE:**

You ask the first person if they can get you a Ferrari for their work car. The response could go something like:

*"While that's a fine car I don't think I have ever seen one in our garage pool of cars but what we do have is a brand new sedan that will save you a lot on fuel and be easier to park."*

The more outrageous the requests the funnier the answers get!

### DE-BRIEF AND REVIEW:

**ASK THE GROUP:**

- Was it difficult to think of positives instead of just going straight to a no?
- What situations can they use this in with customers and discuss scenarios they face
- What can they do to keep this positive focus going?

# PRESSURE COOKER

### OBJECTIVE:

To help the group understand the difference between pressure and stress and identify ways to avoid creating stress in their lives.

| **MATERIAL REQUIRED:** | **TIME REQUIRED:** |
|---|---|
| A bucket or picture of a bucket | 10 – 15 minutes |

### INSTRUCTIONS:

Ask the group what they think is the difference between pressure and stress. Get a few responses and then explain that you'd like to illustrate something for them.

Explain that you have a list of all their names in front of you and that you will randomly pick one and ask them to come to the front and recite a nursery rhyme (or something similar).

Close your eyes and pretend to pick a name at random from an imaginary list. Open your eyes, look down at the list and say: "We're not going to do that".

You will hear sounds of relief from the group!

Explain to the group that they were, at that moment, all under the same pressure. However, some of them had turned it into a stressful situation. Some would be worried they couldn't think of a nursery rhyme, others may even be secretly hoping to get picked as they like the limelight. Whatever they felt, the pressure was the same, and it's what they all did with it that may have turned into stress.

Pressure is external and Stress is internal. The three main stress areas are:

- Internal Stress: Worry
- Environmental Stress: Noise, Crowds, Work
- Chronic Stress: Overworked, too much going on at school, fatigue

Explain that it's really good to have an outlet for stress. Explain that our lives are like a bucket and stuff keeps going into the bucket. At some point the bucket will overflow – that exhibits itself as anger, crying, meltdowns etc. So in order to let stuff out, we need to punch some holes in the bucket. Have a picture or a real bucket to show.

Ask the group for some suggested holes that you can punch in your bucket to relieve some stress?

It's important to understand our own stress relievers for our health's sake.

### DE-BRIEF AND REVIEW:

**ASK THEM:**

- What can you do to avoid these three types of stress?
- If you have one of them surface, what can you do to avoid overflow?

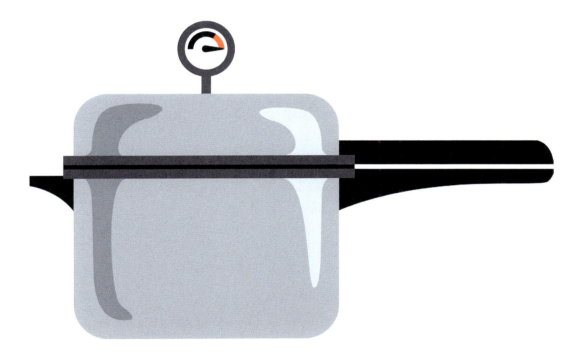

# PROXIMITY

### OBJECTIVE:

A great activity to show the importance of being able to talk to anyone and prospect anywhere.

| **MATERIAL REQUIRED:** | **TIME REQUIRED:** |
|---|---|
| None | 10 - 20 minutes |

### INSTRUCTIONS:

Explain the importance of being able to prospect and talk to anyone anywhere to increase your chances of better sales opportunities.

Give your team the following scenario and then randomly choose someone to start and then take it in turns.

You are heading to a conference where your latest company products are being launched. When you check in, the airline upgrades you! As you excitedly board the plane and sit down you notice the person next to you is one of the high-level executive prospects you have wanted to target for these new products.

The prospect notices you and smiles and says to you "so what do you do?"

Ask each person to pitch their products or business as if they were in that scenario.

### DE-BRIEF AND REVIEW:

When everyone has had a chance at the scenario ask the group:

- How easy was it to come up with a good pitch?
- Discuss the importance of being able to talk to anyone anywhere when you are in sales
- What did you learn from each other's pitches?

Remote Activities For Virtual Teams

# QUESTION STORMING

### OBJECTIVE:

A fun alternative to brainstorming this remote activity can help come up with new solutions and answers.

| MATERIAL REQUIRED: | TIME REQUIRED: |
|---|---|
| None | 15 - 30 minutes |

### INSTRUCTIONS:

**1. START WITH A STATEMENT.**

Instead of starting with a question like, "How can we generate more customers?" it is important to start with a statement like, "We need more customers." A great place to start is with those known truths that you all assume to be foundational. Throughout the process, people often find these to not be true after all.

**2. LIST AS MANY QUESTIONS AS YOU CAN.**

Now that you have your statement, have the team list out as many questions as possible. One very important rule for this phase is that there is no answering of questions allowed. Only questions -- no answers.

At around the 12 minute mark say, "Now that you think you have listed all the possible questions, every team (you can create teams in breakout rooms) needs to write at least 10 more." It's amazing how many questions are created with this simple prompt.

**3. OPEN CLOSED QUESTIONS, AND CLOSE OPEN ONES.**

Now that the list of questions is created, each one is tweaked slightly by either opening or closing it. This creates double the amount of questions (or more) and showcases the importance of nuance. A slight change in wording can result in a completely different question, and therefore research project or answer.

For example, if we go back to the "We need more customers" statement, maybe one of the questions generated was, "How could we make joining us easy?"

That is an open question. To change it to a closed question, it could become, "Is joining us easy?" This is now a 'yes' or 'no' question -- and the experience in answering it would be very different.

**4. PRIORITIZE AND PICK YOUR FAVOURITES.**

Now you have a long list of possible questions from the statement you started with, and lots of reasons to believe it is not necessarily true. Have each member of the team pick their top three questions that they would be

### DE-BRIEF AND REVIEW:

This activity should get a lot of discussion going around the topic you have chosen. You can ask the following questions:

- What surprises came out of that for you?
- What did you enjoy about exploring that topic?
- What other issues / topics can we use that for?

# RANDOM OBJECTS

### OBJECTIVE:

This is an icebreaker activity that can be done any time and helps people get a better understanding of their co-workers.

| MATERIAL REQUIRED: | TIME REQUIRED: |
|---|---|
| Items on desks | 5 – 15 minutes |

### INSTRUCTIONS:

Each person will have a turn at this activity. Ask someone to start off by choosing the most random or unusual item on their desk, wall or in their desk draw and showing the group.

They should then explain the back story of why they have it, where it came from and some information about it.

Depending on the size of the team and time, you could even do a second round of this.

Variations of this means you could ask the person sharing their random object to link it somehow to a company product, service or company value. This could also help solidify the product and company knowledge and values into the team.

### DE-BRIEF AND REVIEW:

**ASK THE GROUP:**

- Who learnt something?
- Were there any common themes?
- How could each object relate to our business in some way?

# RECIPE FOR SUCCESS

### OBJECTIVE:

To help the group share their thoughts and ideas on what makes a team work together successfully and other aspects. A fun session starter.

| **MATERIAL REQUIRED:** | **TIME REQUIRED:** |
|---|---|
| Paper and pen for each person | 10 - 20 minutes |

### INSTRUCTIONS:

Ensure everyone has a pen and paper and give them a time limit to write down their recipe for success. You can ask for more specific recipes like:

- Recipe for being a good team member
- Recipe for being a good friend
- Recipe for being successful at working from home
- Recipe for being a good sale person etc
- Recipe for working in a high performing team

Have everyone share their recipes with the group.

### DE-BRIEF AND REVIEW:

**ASK THE GROUP:**

Ask a few questions like:

- Did we hear similar things mentioned? Why?
- Are you following your own recipe?
- Was there anything you would copy from someone else's recipe? Why?
- What other recipes could we develop?

 PROFESSIONALISM

 EFFICIENCY

 CREATIVITY

 COMMITMENT

# RECOGNITION SPOT

## OBJECTIVE:

To share appreciation for each other by highlighting specific praise for contributions made to the team.

| **MATERIAL REQUIRED:** | **TIME REQUIRED:** |
|---|---|
| None | 5 minutes |

## INSTRUCTIONS:

This activity can be done anytime and works well at the start of a team meeting session.

Allow 5 minutes in total at the start of the session for anyone to recognise someone else in the team for something they have done that has helped them or contributed to the team in a significant way or that has saved someone time etc.

An example might be:

*"I'd like to recognise Sally for showing me how to use the new software properly. She was patient with me and now I get it. I feel so much more confident as a result. Thanks Sally."*

You don't have to go round the group – this is just for highlights and you may only have two or three suggestions.

Don't force this and don't expect each person to nominate someone for recognition. You don't want to dilute the experience.

## DE-BRIEF AND REVIEW:

- Thank those that have recognised others and share your appreciation for the value everyone brings.

# REVEALING TEAM

### OBJECTIVE:

To help groups or teams bond together and have fun while learning about each other. A fun trust building activity.

| **MATERIAL REQUIRED:** | **TIME REQUIRED:** |
|---|---|
| Pre work for gathering information and a quiz platform like Kahoot! | 20 minutes |

### INSTRUCTIONS:

Gather a few random facts about each person in the team or group. Prepare a quiz based on this random fact with the object of the group to guess who the fact belongs to. The more random the facts the better. Ensure you have permission to share these facts with the wider group.

Using a quiz platform like Kahoot! Is great for this as you can add 4 team name options for each fact and the team guess live and get scored on correct answers as well as speed of answer.

Ensure each team member is the correct answer at least once during the quiz.

Run the quiz over your remote team platform. Allow the group to enjoy the experience.

### DE-BRIEF AND REVIEW:

- See how the group are feeling. Ask them if they had discovered any surprises. You may like to offer some question time about one another based on the facts.
- You could suggest that each person shares something about the random fact too.

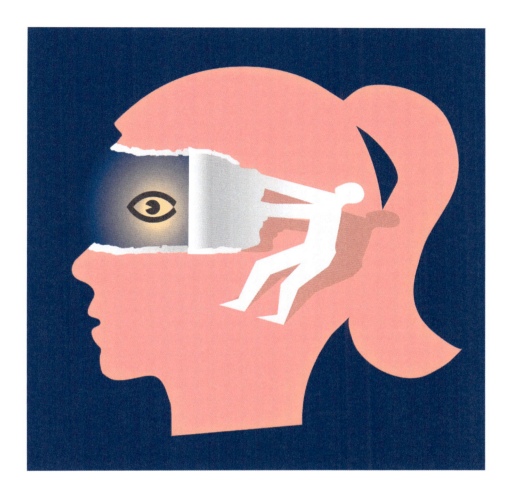

# ROCK PAPER SCISSORS

### OBJECTIVE:

A bit of fun to get the energy going with the team and work under pressure.

| MATERIAL REQUIRED: | TIME REQUIRED: |
|---|---|
| None | 10 – 15 minutes |

### INSTRUCTIONS:

Two people will square off at the start and the winner goes on to play the next person on the team, and so on. It's a great way to test people's reflexes, responsiveness, and encourage spontaneity. It can even be a great warm up before a brainstorm.

Rock, Paper, Scissors is a widely-known traditional game so explanation shouldn't be needed but do a quick review in case:

- Rock beats scissors
- Scissors beats paper
- Paper beats rock

See how many rounds a person can win to be crowned the champion.

### DE-BRIEF AND REVIEW:

Discuss as a group how they found coping under pressure when their turn was coming.

You could discuss strategy for this game. There are some strategies that people use to defeat opponents. One winning strategy is to choose the next hand based on what would have beaten the hand your opponent just used. So if they used Rock, choose Paper next. When you win, switch to the hand that would beat the hand you just played.

# SALES STAMINA

### OBJECTIVE:

A good way to test knowledge of products or co-workers in a fun and challenging way.

| MATERIAL REQUIRED: | TIME REQUIRED: |
|---|---|
| Selection of random products on cards | 10 – 30 minutes depending on size of the group. |

### INSTRUCTIONS:

The aim of the activity is to build sales stamina and the ability to think on your feet. Randomly choose a person to start and they select any card – you turn over the card they choose and announce the first feature or benefit of the product you then go round each person in the group until someone can't think of something and they drop out. The winner gets to choose the next card and continues on.

It could go something like this: A marker is chosen.

1. It's colourful
2. It's easy to use
3. It's waterproof
4. It can be carried anywhere
5. It writes on anything

You change this to using your own products or services.

### DE-BRIEF AND REVIEW:

Discuss thinking on your feet and features and benefits of products / services.

# SELF-DISCLOSURE

### OBJECTIVE:

This activity is great for the start of a session and as an icebreaker for new teams Great for existing teams to learn more of each other too.

| MATERIAL REQUIRED: | TIME REQUIRED: |
|---|---|
| People need to have their wallets / purses handy | 10 – 20 minutes |

### INSTRUCTIONS:

Tell people to take two items out of their wallets, purses or pockets. Ask them to introduce themselves using those two items. They will use credit cards, lipstick, photos, handkerchiefs, store cards etc

Give everyone 1 minute to share their introductions.

Examples: "This is my handkerchief. When I was very young, I used to have a handkerchief with me at all times. I would chew on it and it was my comforter."

"This is a photo of my daughter when she was very young. It reminds me of simpler times and how fast moments go by. I have four children by the way."

If teams are already familiar with each other, explain that this is a great way to learn something we might not already know about each other.

### DE-BRIEF AND REVIEW:

**ASK THE GROUP:**
- Did anyone learn something new?
- Was it hard to think of something to say?
- Did anyone realise they should have a clean out of their wallets?

# SILVER LINING

### OBJECTIVE:

This activity is a great start to a virtual meeting. It helps to put people on the same wavelength and look for the positive.

| MATERIAL REQUIRED: | TIME REQUIRED: |
|---|---|
| None | 5 – 10 minutes |

### INSTRUCTIONS:

Each person takes a minute to share a challenge they are facing either at work or non-work related. They then share something positive they have found in that challenge.

If time, have each person share a work related and non-work related example.

Always start with the challenge (the cloud) then add the silver lining.

Examples:

*"I lost a big customer last week. One that had been with us for a while. The silver lining is that I have had to do more 'cold calling' and as a result I picked up two new accounts yesterday and they have the potential to be bigger than the customer I lost."*

*"The weather has been so bad lately that I haven't been able to go fishing. The silver lining though is that it has helped me get some jobs finished that I haven't prioritised and it feels great!"*

If anyone struggles to find a silver lining, ask the group for assistance. Be careful not to probe into any personal areas that may be sensitive or inappropriate.

### DE-BRIEF AND REVIEW:

- Thank the group for sharing examples. Help them see that we can look at positive angles in negative situations.

# SIMONE SAYS

## OBJECTIVE:

To help participants pay attention to a changed set of rules and listen to instructions.

| **MATERIAL REQUIRED:** | **TIME REQUIRED:** |
| --- | --- |
| None | 10 - 15 minutes |

## INSTRUCTIONS:

Select a person to act as Simone (subtle name change from the familiar Simon). It's Simone's job to call out simple commands for others to follow. Videos need to be enabled for this activity.

If Simone calls out a command which begins with "Simone Says…" then the participants must NOT obey the command.

If the command does not begin with "Simone says…" then they MUST obey it or are eliminated from the game.

The aim is for Simone to get everyone out.

You can repeat with a new Simone after a time limit or if everyone is out.

Variations of this could be that you change out the name 'Simone' for the name of your CEO or have two Simone's going alternating commands – simulating different messages.

## DE-BRIEF AND REVIEW:

**ASK THEM:**

- How was it to play the game in the opposite way to normal?
- What was it like to be eliminated from the game?
- What have we changed at work lately?
- How difficult was it to give commands differently?
- What can we apply to our roles?

# SKETCH THIS

### OBJECTIVE:

To show the importance of two-way communication as well as the uniqueness of personal interpretation.

**MATERIAL REQUIRED:**

Paper and pen or pencil for each person

**TIME REQUIRED:**

15 minutes

### INSTRUCTIONS:

Have a volunteer in the group to pick an object or a drawing and then describe it to the rest of the group. It's important that the volunteer not display the image or object at all to the rest of the group.

Get them to carefully describe it to the others so that they can draw a replica on a piece of paper.

The group is not allowed to ask questions or get the volunteer to repeat any of the steps. There is to be no communication the other way – just from the volunteer.

When they are finished, give the group a few seconds to add finishing touches and then reveal one by one. Don't reveal the original image or object until the end.

### DE-BRIEF AND REVIEW:

**ASK THE GROUP:**

- What was it was like to participate in this exercise?
- What would have made it easier?
- How similar was their sketch to the original?
- What can we learn from this? (Ensure the points are made concerning – two way communications is always better to clarify and that individual interpretation can be a problem if you want consistency).

Discuss the responsibility is normally on both the sender of the message or information and the receiver to both clarify understanding.

# SMILING CHAT

### OBJECTIVE:

To start a session off with positives and help the group feel grateful. It will also help groups gain a greater appreciation of everyday things and create an air of positivity.

| MATERIAL REQUIRED: | TIME REQUIRED: |
|---|---|
| None | 10 minutes |

### INSTRUCTIONS:

Using the technology chat feature of whatever you're using, ask each person to post a chat to everyone of one thing that made them smile today (or yesterday or this week).

Allow everyone time to read through the chats as they come in.

You may like to read them aloud or just allow everyone the personal time to read and digest.

This isn't a competition but rather a 'share to all' and 'hear from all' opportunity.

Variations of this activity could include sharing verbally the thing that has made them smile.

You could also collect the transcript and send it to everyone or create an image with all the smiley comments on them.

### DE-BRIEF AND REVIEW:

- This will start your session off on a high. You could ask people how they're feeling.
- Ask the group if they would like to do this again and what variations they can think of.

# SOMETHING IN COMMON

### OBJECTIVE:

A great way for team members to get to know each other and share experiences.

| MATERIAL REQUIRED: | TIME REQUIRED: |
| --- | --- |
| None | 15 – 25 minutes depending on size of the group. |

### INSTRUCTIONS:

Explain that when the activity starts you will choose someone at random and they then have to call out another team member's name and say something they have in common with that person.

This could be the same letter of their name, they started together in the company, they have the same pets etc.

Then the second person who was mentioned has to call out a different team member's name and say what they have in common.

This continues until all team members have had a turn calling out someone else's name.

### DE-BRIEF AND REVIEW:

- Discuss how much they know about each other and how as a team they have things in common.

# SOMETHING'S AFOOT

### OBJECTIVE:

A great energizer to discuss about change and that there are some things you can't actually alter. It will help people experience a strange phenomenon.

| MATERIAL REQUIRED: | TIME REQUIRED: |
| --- | --- |
| None | 5 minutes |

### INSTRUCTIONS:

Ask each person to raise their right foot in the air and draw clockwise circles.

While doing this, ask them to raise their right hand and draw the number 6 in the air.

Their right foot will automatically change direction. There is nothing you can do to stop it.

### DE-BRIEF AND REVIEW:

**ASK THEM:**

- How weird was that?
- What applications are there?

Focus on the point that no matter what you do, you can't alter this phenomenon. It's a bit like some things in life – no matter what you do, you can't change them.

Are there any aspects like that in our roles?

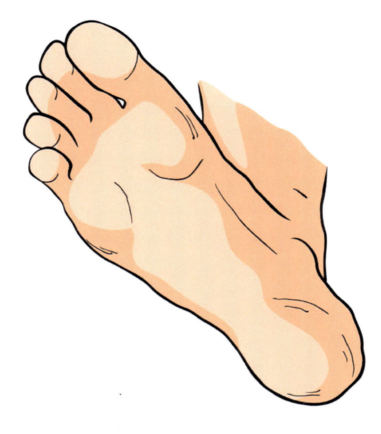

# SONGFEST

### OBJECTIVE:

This activity is a bit of fun and can be used as an energizer at the start of a session or to have some fun as a team.

| MATERIAL REQUIRED: | TIME REQUIRED: |
| --- | --- |
| Prepared list of words | 15 - 20 minutes |

### INSTRUCTIONS:

Prepare a list of words – common words work best. Explain to the group that once you have said a word, the group needs to think of a song that has that word in the title. They should then type 'X" in the chat window so you know who is first.

Ask the person to reveal that song title. You could offer bonus points if they sing the line that was in their head that reminded them of that song.

Choose another word and repeat.

Variations of this could include using product or service names or words from the company values. This is a way to help promote product and service knowledge as well as organisational information and values.

### DE-BRIEF AND REVIEW:

**ASK THE GROUP:**

- Who learnt something new?
- What was your plan to try and get points?

# STRESS TEMPERATURE

## OBJECTIVE:

A good way for the team to share where their stress levels are at.

| MATERIAL REQUIRED: | TIME REQUIRED: |
|---|---|
| A pre-drawn thermometer empty | 10 - 15 minutes |

## INSTRUCTIONS:

This is a simple way to measure the stress levels of your group. All you will need to do is draw a picture of a thermometer on a piece of paper or have one drawn online.

When you begin your session, start off with asking your group what their stress levels are. They will then need to tell you by you starting at the bottom and slowly raising your pen (or if you can share your screen have them mark for themselves on the pre drawn picture online) until they say stop and you mark and write their name.

Written on the picture of the thermometer at the top can be, 'About to explode' and at the bottom 'Chilled and Relaxed'.

There are many techniques and ways to manage stress simply, but when we are in the middle of a stressful moment, we tend to forget what we can do to help. The best way to tackle this is to prepare and practice stress management techniques, ensuring they will harness these techniques when necessary.

## DE-BRIEF AND REVIEW:

**ASK THE GROUP:**

- Who knew other team members felt stressed?
- Does it help reduce their stress knowing they aren't the only ones?
- As a team, what can they do to help support each other?

# SUNGLASSES

### OBJECTIVE:

To illustrate that our attitudes can be changed and dependent on our approach.

| MATERIAL REQUIRED: | TIME REQUIRED: |
|---|---|
| A pair of sunglasses | 5 - 10 minutes |

### INSTRUCTIONS:

Put on a pair of sunglasses and just look around the group.

Ask the group who wears sunglasses from time to time.

Ask the group why they change sunglasses (They break, get lost, go out of fashion, get scratched)

Focus on the scratched lens. That's what you see when you put on those sunglasses – it obscures our view somewhat. Explain to the group that in our lives, we see things in a particular way – like wearing sunglasses. During our life we pick up scratches on our lenses due to experiences we have:

- We get a boss – all bosses are like them – scratch on the lens
- We meet someone from America – all Americans are like them – scratch on the lens
- We get asked to do a project – all projects are like that – scratch on the lens
- We speak to a customer who has English as a second language – all those who have English as a second language are like them – scratch on the lens

### DE-BRIEF AND REVIEW:

It's not until we take off the sunglasses that we see more clearly. So, occasionally, take off those sunglasses of life and look at things without a pre-determined view or prejudice. It can make all the difference when dealing with customers and colleagues. Ask some questions:

- What are some prejudices we may have with customers? Colleagues? Suppliers?
- How can we overcome those prejudices?

# SUPERLATIVES

### OBJECTIVE:

To help groups or teams bond together and have fun. To help people think about the group individuals and be creative. This activity could be run over a one period.

| MATERIAL REQUIRED: | TIME REQUIRED: |
|---|---|
| None | 10 minutes for the reveal |
|  | 1 hour to 1 day to run |

### INSTRUCTIONS:

Put a list of superlatives together. A superlative is a way of describing something to the greatest or least degree. For example, 'The person most likely to be famous'. Ask for suggestions and create a list of say 20 superlatives that you can send out as a list at the start of the day. Give them a specific time scale to complete.

Have each person complete their list by voting for who in the team or group would be suit teach superlative in their opinion and send it back to you. Total up the vote and then do a group reveal of who had the most votes for each superlative.

Some examples you could use:
- Person most likely to deal with a difficult customer today
- Person most likely to take the most toilet breaks today
- Person least likely to start work on time today

You could do some prizes or booby prizes. Perhaps the person with the most votes overall gets to run the next activity.

An activity like this can be seen as a team builder or a reward activity to reveal at the end of the shift.

### DE-BRIEF AND REVIEW:

Explain that activities like this don't take long and help to bond the group.

**ASK THE GROUP:**
- Who learnt something?
- Were there any surprises?
- What are some other superlatives we could use next time?
- Who had fun doing that?

# Comparatives & Superlatives

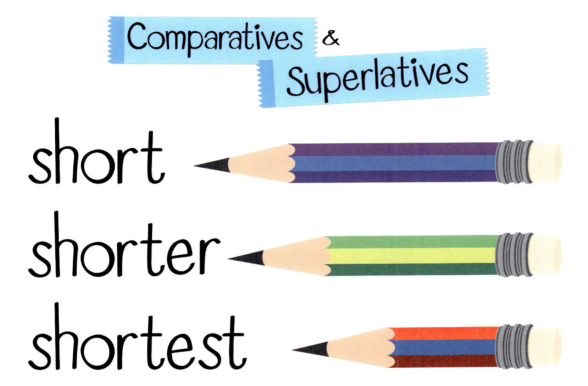

short

shorter

shortest

# SWITCHING SIDES

### OBJECTIVE:

A great way to discover different outcomes from different leadership styles.

| **MATERIAL REQUIRED:** | **TIME REQUIRED:** |
| --- | --- |
| None | 10 - 30 minutes |

### INSTRUCTIONS:

The aim of this activity is for participants to reflect upon different leadership styles and come up with a list of actual workplace scenarios which would need them / a leader to have to leave a natural leadership style for one that is more effective for the situation and therefore to 'switch sides'.

Ask the teams to take one style of leadership on a style like autocratic, delegative, democratic. Then, allow the groups to come up with real actual work situations for which employing the leadership style would be disastrous.

Ask the groups to discuss the results as a team in a break out room. As a whole group, review the results and discuss the outcomes.

### DE-BRIEF AND REVIEW:

**ASK THE GROUP:**

- Who learnt something new about adapting styles?
- What was the most surprising fact when looking at real life situations?

# SYNCHRONISED CLAPPING

## OBJECTIVE:

To demonstrate that people generally want to comply and that leaders don't have to micro manage every instruction.

**MATERIAL REQUIRED:**
None

**TIME REQUIRED:**
3 minutes

## INSTRUCTIONS:

Explain to the group that you would like them to all clap their hands in unison. Tell them to start clapping and get into the same rhythm.

The group will start to clap and in a very short space of time they will naturally form a rhythm that they will all be in sync with.

Allow them to clap in that rhythm for a few seconds before you stop them.

## DE-BRIEF AND REVIEW:

- Ask the group how easy it was to get into the same rhythm. Was there anyone who wanted to break the rhythm – why or why not?
- Explain that for most people, wanting to comply with instruction is quite natural.
- Discuss that when you give instruction, it isn't necessary to provide micro-management on every action. You didn't need to coach them on how to clap or how to get in time – the group just did it naturally.
- Not everything needs step by step instructions and you can trust people to get on with things.

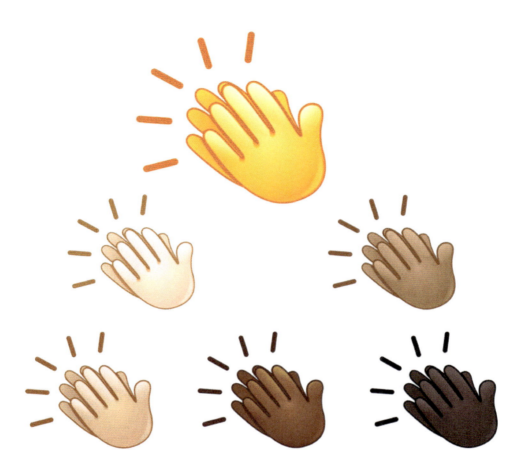

# TEAM SCAVENGER HUNT

### OBJECTIVE:

This activity is best done by giving the group some time to complete. You may consider doing this over a day or a week depending on the opportunities the team have to interact. You can then do a reveal at a nominated group session.

| MATERIAL REQUIRED: | TIME REQUIRED: |
| --- | --- |
| Pen and paper for everyone and pre-prepared list of items to hunt for | 5 - 10 minutes during a session reveal plus at least a day to complete the activity. |

### INSTRUCTIONS:

Prepare a list of items for the team to find out about their group like:

- Person with the most siblings
- Person who has travelled to the most countries
- Person who has worked at the company the longest
- Person who has met someone famous (BONUS: Who was it?)
- Person who knows the most languages etc

Invite the group to complete their scavenger hunt throughout the day or week or whatever timescale you're using by asking questions each time they interact with another member of the team. You could invite each person to submit three items to go on the hunt list and choose one from each person (some duplicates will be likely).

Do a reveal at a group online session. There is the potential to do prizes for the most correct responses.

### DE-BRIEF AND REVIEW:

**ASK THE GROUP:**

- What did we learn about each other?
- What was your strategy for finding out the responses?
- What would we like to see on the next list?

For Virtual Teams

# STORYTELLING

...actice listening to what is being said and to learn ways to build on ideas.

| MATERIAL REQUIRED: | TIME REQUIRED: |
|---|---|
| None | 10 - 15 minutes |

## INSTRUCTIONS:

Team storytelling is a fun improvisation activity that can be done anywhere and is especially great for remote teams as a way to interact. It's a great way to get people to listen while someone else is speaking and is a great team building activity for teams who are working together in a virtual environment.

Start by asking someone to say an adjective like 'Frustrated'.

Next ask someone to say an animal like 'Elephant'.

Someone then starts the story about the topic – in this case a frustrated elephant by saying one word to get the team started.

Decide on an order and each person then adds one word to the story in turn and so on until the story ends.

## DE-BRIEF AND REVIEW:

You may need to give a key word to use as the ending such as 'End' or you may like to give a time limit and gave someone wrap it up.

The group should enjoy the activity.

### ASK THE GROUP:

- What did we learn about each other?
- Was it difficult when it came to your turn?
- Did you zone out at all?
- What did you learn about listening?
- Did you feel like you owned part of the story?

# THE POINTER

### OBJECTIVE:

To illustrate that we can always achieve a little more than we first think we can. There's always something we can add to our first effort. This is also a good exercise to do to get the group energized.

| **MATERIAL REQUIRED:** | **TIME REQUIRED:** |
|---|---|
| None | 5 minutes |

### INSTRUCTIONS:

The participants will need a bit of room for this, so explain that at the start. Good to keep video views on for this one too. You should be involved and demonstrate as you go.

Ask everyone to stand up and place their feet firmly on the floor and remain there for the entire exercise.

Ask them to twist around and point their index finger as far as they can, taking note of where they reached.

Now ask the group to swing their hips in a flowing motion and point their index finger looking in that direction and repeat 5 times.

On the last swing, ask the participants to see how far they can point. How does it compare with the initial pointing?

### DE-BRIEF AND REVIEW:

**ASK THE GROUP:**

- How much further could they point?
- What made the difference?
- How could we apply that to our roles?

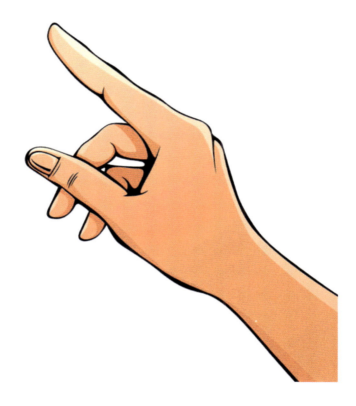

# THIS YEAR

### OBJECTIVE:

This icebreaker is a great way to get people engaged at the start of a session. It's also a way to get people thinking on their feet and to learn something about each other.

| MATERIAL REQUIRED: | TIME REQUIRED: |
|---|---|
| Bag of coins or something with a year on it | 5 - 10 minutes |

### INSTRUCTIONS:

With a bag of coins or some other method of randomising recent years, pull a coin out at random and assign the year date on it to a person, then repeat until everyone has a year.

You could randomise a bag full of pieces of paper with a year on each one and do the same thing.

If this is a new group, you may like to use this as a way of introducing each other:

Name, basic other information you want each person to share and then:

Share something significant that happened to them in the year they have been assigned.

Allow each person to be able to share the significant thing for them in their specific year.

Give them a few minutes to think before sharing. If someone can't think of anything, ask them to describe what was going on in their life – where were they living, where did they work, what was their favourite movie etc…

### DE-BRIEF AND REVIEW:

**ASK THE GROUP:**
- Why is it important to know things about each other?
- How difficult or easy was it to share something about your year?

# THREE TRUTHS, ONE LIE

### OBJECTIVE:

To have a bit of fun on a conference all and practice being observant to what is going on around you. It also helps to prove the point that people will watch even the smallest things.

| MATERIAL REQUIRED: | TIME REQUIRED: |
|---|---|
| None | 10 - 15 minutes plus some time for participants to prepare |

### INSTRUCTIONS:

Host a video conference and ask each remote employee to tell three truths and one lie about themselves. Give them some time to prepare for this – maybe a day in advance or at least a few minutes during the session.

Keep the lie realistic so it won't be so easy for everyone to guess. The other group members need to guess which the lie was and whoever guesses right gains points.

Keep a score going and even roll it over to the next week / call to keep a scoreboard!

### DE-BRIEF AND REVIEW:

**ASK THE GROUP:**

Playing this game helps to get rid of any awkwardness as it is light and fun. Plus, it is a great way to get to know one another, especially things that aren't common knowledge even among teams.

# TIME WASTERS

### OBJECTIVE:

A good activity for managers but could be adapted for all teams. To illustrate how to work together as well as be aware for what takes up manager's time the most. Variations noted could be used to build top 10 lists of a variety of topics which help to understand your business better.

| MATERIAL REQUIRED: | TIME REQUIRED: |
|---|---|
| Use breakout rooms if available. List of Time Wasters prepared for you | 15 – 20 minutes |

### INSTRUCTIONS:

Have the list of time wasters ready. For this example, you can use time wasters for managers – a top 10 list prepared from professional research:

1. Crises
2. Telephone calls
3. Poor planning
4. Attempting to do too much
5. Drip-in visitors
6. Poor delegation
7. Personal disorganisation
8. Lack of self-discipline
9. Inability to say 'no'
10. Procrastination

Split the group in to breakout rooms so they can discuss and come up with their top 10 list of time wasters for managers. When the time is up, get the groups to share their responses and you can then reveal the 'top ten' list you have.

If you can't use breakout rooms, then give the task to individuals to do.

Variations could include any research based or just lists you hope to compile for Time Wasters, Customer Complaints, Reasons Customers Say No etc.

### DE-BRIEF AND REVIEW:

**ASK THE GROUP:**

- How did you come up with the answers?
- Why is this information useful?
- Did it help being in / not being in a group to work through this?
- Which of these time wasters do you need to focus on and overcome first?

You can then work on an action list or get them to pick the one they believe they don't do and the one they need to work on most.

# TOP 5

### OBJECTIVE:

To help the group focus on the positives of certain situations. To also help the group practice creativity skills.

| MATERIAL REQUIRED: | TIME REQUIRED: |
|---|---|
| Paper and pen for each person | 10 – 20 minutes<br><br>Could also be done as a day-long activity |

### INSTRUCTIONS:

Prepare some categories to give people to work on. These categories could be the same for each person or you could provide separate ones for each. You could also ask the group to come up with categories.

The idea is to have each person come up with their top 5 reasons for each category.

Some examples could be:

- Top 5 reasons you like to work at this organisation
- Top 5 reasons you like to live in the city you do
- Top 5 reasons this group is the best team in the business
- Top 5 reasons your country is the best in the world

Allow everyone to share their reasons with the group for their categories.

You could run this as a longer term activity and have the group work on their lists throughout the day and share at the end of the day.

### DE-BRIEF AND REVIEW:

Discuss how important it is to know why we do things. Making a list like this can help cement in the reasons. It may also identify that change is needed.

**ASK THE GROUP:**

- Was it easy to come up with 5 reasons?
- Why may it be hard – what could that tell us?

# TRAFFIC LIGHT REVIEW

### OBJECTIVE:

A useful activity to use at the end of a session. It helps people focus on the application of what has been covered and discussed. It will also provide a good catalyst for discussion for a participant and their manager when they return to the workplace.

| MATERIAL REQUIRED: | TIME REQUIRED: |
|---|---|
| Paper and pen for each person | 5 minutes |

### INSTRUCTIONS:

As a result of what has been discussed in the online session, ask the participants to consider the following:

- What are two things you will start doing as a result of your experience in the session today?
- What are two things you will stop doing?
- What are two things you will continue to do?

This could be used for a coaching session online, a team meeting or a training session.

You could suggest one thing for each part if you feel two is too many.

### DE-BRIEF AND REVIEW:

- Invite the group to share some of their commitments.

# UNFORTUNATELY FORTUNATELY

## OBJECTIVE:

To help the group see that there are always two ways to look at things. This is an attitude energizer that helps people think on their feet, get engaged and look for positives.

| **MATERIAL REQUIRED:** | **TIME REQUIRED:** |
| --- | --- |
| None | 5 - 10 minutes |

## INSTRUCTIONS:

Organise the group into an order. Agree on names alphabetically or some other way so everyone knows who follows after whom. This is a variation of standing together in a circle in person. This works well if there is an odd number. You may want to start and step out if there is an even number of people.

Explain to the group that we will start with a statement and then the first person will say something about that statement beginning with "Unfortunately…". The next person then says something about that last statement beginning with "Fortunately…". You then alternate around the group with "Unfortunately" then "Fortunately". You can keep doing rounds or throw in a new statement.

For example:

Statement: We just bought a new cat.

First person could say: "Unfortunately it isn't house trained yet"

Next person could say: "Fortunately we have wooden floors so it's easy to clean up"

Next person: "Unfortunately I'm the only one at home at the moment so I'm doing all the clean-up."

And so on….

## DE-BRIEF AND REVIEW:

**ASK THEM:**

- What does this activity teach us?
- How easy was it to find a contrary statement?
- How can we apply this to our roles?

# VALUE APPS

### OBJECTIVE:

To help internalise the values of the organisation and energise the team. Variations mean this could also be done as a review activity for the session.

| MATERIAL REQUIRED: | TIME REQUIRED: |
|---|---|
| None | 10 - 15 minutes |

### INSTRUCTIONS:

Have a list of the company values available. Divide the values amongst the people present in your team. If you have 20 people and 4 values then have 5 people on each values team.

Give the teams a few minutes to chat together. If remotely, this could be done in a separate breakout room. If this is impossible then consider giving each person in the team a specific APP to work with.

The idea is to come up with something related to the value using a popular APP. For example:

YouTUBE, Spotify, Snapchat etc. Have the team or team member come up with the following:

e.g. Spotify – a song that includes the value in it or that represents the value. Or for Snapchat – an image or drawing that encapsulates the value. Pick an app or have the team come up with the apps. Or for YouTUBE – a quick video, story, example or skit that demonstrates the value.

Finally, use the pun – how can they 'APP'ly the value and get people to share one thing they can do to demonstrate that value in their role.

Consider repeating the activity on other days with a different value per team or concentrate on just one value for the session to really help to internalise it.

A variation on this activity is for you to use the APPS component as a review of components of the session.

### DE-BRIEF AND REVIEW:

- The group should be quite energised during and after the activity. You could ask them to record what they will be doing to demonstrate the value. Ask the group to share how they are feeling. What did they learn?
- Could we do this for other things like customer needs or products?

# VIRTUAL CHARADES

### OBJECTIVE:

This is a team building activity that can be used to also develop knowledge of products and services.

| **MATERIAL REQUIRED:** | **TIME REQUIRED:** |
|---|---|
| None | 15 – 20 minutes |

### INSTRUCTIONS:

Ensure everyone has access to video for this activity. Have someone start off with an assigned word or phrase, product, service etc to act out for the rest of the group to guess. The person has one minute to get someone to guess. The person that guesses correctly and the person acting out get a point each if guessed within one minute. If the guess occurs within 30 seconds, both get 2 points.

Decide if the next person is the guesser or the next in line.

Try using the chat feature for the guessing. Have someone monitor the chat for the first correct guess to come up.

Total up scores for a winner.

Variations can include fun topics, products, people in the business etc.

### DE-BRIEF AND REVIEW:

**ASK THE GROUP:**
- What did we learn?
- What other topics can we use?

# VIRTUAL FITNESS

### OBJECTIVE:

This can be varied in lots of ways and is done over a time period. The results are shared in a group session.

| MATERIAL REQUIRED: | TIME REQUIRED: |
| --- | --- |
| Health tracking mechanism for each person (normally a phone with health monitor) | 5 – 10 minutes result session<br><br>1 – 2 week running period |

### INSTRUCTIONS:

Have the group agree on a fitness challenge for a period of time. Ensure it is something that is measurable, recordable and doable for all team members.

For example, have a fitness challenge to do as many steps per day over a 2 week period.

At an agreed starting time and session reveal, share results by showing them on screen.

You can either then organise a prize for the winner or you can organise a prize for everyone who achieves the goal. Having a prize for everyone that completes is a great way of motivating as it doesn't just highlight one person.

As this is a longer term activity, it can be something you can do follow up with daily. Part of your daily check-ins could be devoted to how the progress is going. You could post updates as you go.

### DE-BRIEF AND REVIEW:

- Discuss how everyone did. What did people do to complete the challenge? Did they feel good? Has it given them the desire to keep going? What changes have they noticed?
- What can we do together next?

# VIRTUAL PICTIONARY

### OBJECTIVE:

This fun activity can be used to improve product / service knowledge or just a fun activity to build team understanding.

| MATERIAL REQUIRED: | TIME REQUIRED: |
| --- | --- |
| Annotation component on your conference call | 20 minutes |

### INSTRUCTIONS:

Based on the popular board game of Pictionary, utilise your conferencing's ability to share screen and annotate on a virtual whiteboard. Popular conferencing software like Zoom has this as standard or you could even use Microsoft Paint and share screen.

Have someone draw something on the screen and the rest of the group has to guess what it is. Have a timer going. The person that guesses it correctly and the artist both get a point if guessed within a minute, 2 points if guessed within 30 seconds. Tally a score and give a prize to the winner.

Use products or services as the clues or widen it to other topics to suit the group.

### DE-BRIEF AND REVIEW:

**ASK THEM:**

- What did we learn?
- What else could we do this for?

# VIRTUAL RACE

### OBJECTIVE:

This is a fun activity to be used as an energizer at the start of a session.

| MATERIAL REQUIRED: | TIME REQUIRED: |
|---|---|
| None | 10 – 15 minutes |

### INSTRUCTIONS:

There are two ways to run this activity. Firstly, you are looking for the first person to appear with the named object on the screen with them.

Instructions: Explain to the group that the first person to show themselves with the object you mention on the screen wins a point. Then one by one name a number of objects pausing in between to confirm the winner of the point. The winner is the first person you see with the named object. You must pay attention to all screens. There may be some dead-heats and you will share the point between them. Tally points after a specific time or number of objects. A prize for the winner is customary.

Examples:
- A stapler
- Pair of glasses
- A pet
- Family member etc

Make the items a little harder as you go.

The second way to run this activity to is to give a time limit for them to get the object and show it. If they fail to do so in the time limit they are eliminated. Make the objects more difficult or the time limit shorter as you go until you end up with one person who is the winner.

### DE-BRIEF AND REVIEW:

**ASK THE GROUP:**
- How was it?
- Did you have a plan for finding objects quickly?
- What were you hoping we'd ask for that wasn't?

# WHAT ONE QUESTION?

## OBJECTIVE:

Identifying really good questions in a sales situation.

| MATERIAL REQUIRED: | TIME REQUIRED: |
|---|---|
| None | 15 – 30 minutes depending on size of the group. |

## INSTRUCTIONS:

You ask the team to work together to identify the one question they could use to determine someone's suitability for a specific situation, such as leading the company, joining the team, babysitting a child, or anything else.

Coming up with one perfect question is much harder than building a list of good questions – and it's a great skill to have in sales.

You could make it more specific to your business by coming up with a list such as what's one question for:

- Identifying the perfect prospect
- Getting the timing right on a sale
- Matching the right product or solution to a customer

## DE-BRIEF AND REVIEW:

Sometimes it's harder to identify really targeted and resourceful questions than we realise.

**ASK THE GROUP:**

- What is a question you have heard or used in the past that has been perfect for certain situation?
- What helps to make a really good powerful question?

# WHAT'S IN A NAME?

### OBJECTIVE:

This activity helps the group to learn about themselves and others in the group as well as the potential to identify researching skills.

| MATERIAL REQUIRED: | TIME REQUIRED: |
|---|---|
| None | 10 – 15 minutes |

### INSTRUCTIONS:

You may want to give some notice for this activity. The idea is to have each group member share the meaning of their name. You may want to ask two things:

- Why did your parents call you the names(s) they did?
- What does your name mean?

You could also add the last name into the equation to identify the meaning of that too.

Most people will need some research time for this, so either set the task the day before or give them a few minutes during the session as a break-out time and then restart the session and discuss.

Allow each person the chance to share their names' meanings.

Variations could include names of businesses, competitors, cities, countries etc.

### DE-BRIEF AND REVIEW:

Discuss the fact that normally names have meanings to them and the reasons we have been named has some significance. You could ask:

- Who learnt something new about themselves?
- Was it difficult to discover the meaning or reason for your name?
- Do we know why our company is called by its name? What is the significance of that?

# WHERE'S WOTSIT?

### OBJECTIVE:

This activity can be run during a session. No real time limit is needed. The idea is to have people test their observation and creative skills.

| **MATERIAL REQUIRED:** | **TIME REQUIRED:** |
|---|---|
| A similar object or picture for each person | No limit required |

### INSTRUCTIONS:

Before you can run this activity, you will need to provide everyone with the same item or picture or have them print off something that you send them.

Instruct each team member to hide in plain sight the item somewhere than can be seen during their video conference session. This will test their creative skills – not making it obvious where it is showing.

The other team members then try to find where the item is in each person's video screen. This is the observation skills part. A little like the famous 'Where's Wally?' series but using something relevant to the group. If you have products small enough you could even vary it by placing them randomly and seeing how many people can find them.

Use the chat feature to record people's answers so you have a trail of who was first.

### DE-BRIEF AND REVIEW:

**ASK THEM:**

- Who had the most creative place?
- What variations could we do with this?
- Can we relate this to our business?

# WHOSE OFFICE IS IT?

### OBJECTIVE:

To help with team bonding and as a great Icebreaker at the start of a session.

| **MATERIAL REQUIRED:** | **TIME REQUIRED:** |
|---|---|
| None | 10 minutes |

### INSTRUCTIONS:

Before running a session, have your team members send a photo of their home offices / workspaces.

When everyone is online say you are going to show the pictures one at a time of someone's office and if it's yours not to call out. Take one picture at a time and hold it up for the rest of the team to guess. Have everyone guess whose workspace is whose.

Keep the game going with photos of everyone's coffee mugs, desktop backgrounds, or the view outside their window.

This can also be expanded to include random pictures of your company or products to keep people guessing!

### DE-BRIEF AND REVIEW:

**ASK THE GROUP:**

- How easy was to identify each other's workspaces and why? How well do your team members know each other?
- How well do they know their products?

# WORD BUILDER

### OBJECTIVE:

This is a great brain activating game to help start a session. Variations could be used to help cement in product knowledge.

| **MATERIAL REQUIRED:** | **TIME REQUIRED:** |
|---|---|
| None | 10 - 15 minutes |

### INSTRUCTIONS:

Explain to the group that you will be sharing groups of letters and they will need to write down as many words they can think of that utilise those letters. Decide whether the letters need to be in order or not.

You decide the difficulty by using more letters and choosing an order.

You could start with three letters either at random or pre-decided like E M T.

The group then has to come up with as many words as they can think of using those letters (in order or not depending on what you have decided). For example: EMPATHY uses all three letters in order.

You may even vary this by suggesting product names beginning with a specific letter. For example, '"list all products we have beginning with the letter 'T'"

Always give a time frame, and then have the group share back.

### DE-BRIEF AND REVIEW:

**ASK THE GROUP:**

- How hard was it?
- Was it easier after you got started or after a few rounds?
- How could we vary this up some more?

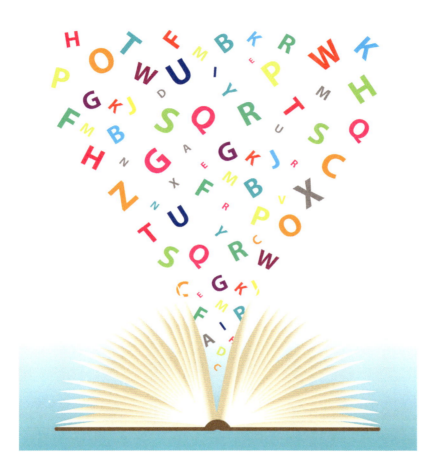

# ZAP!

## OBJECTIVE:

This activity is lots of fun and can help develop product knowledge or knowledge of other topics.

| MATERIAL REQUIRED: | TIME REQUIRED: |
|---|---|
| Pre prepared questions and Zap! cards. | 20 - 30 minutes |

## INSTRUCTIONS:

For this activity, you need to create some prepared score cards that you can use in a virtual grid. These cards can be anything you like but help to create the fun of the game. You create a grid size that you want – 25 squares for example and have a card for each number.

Cards should reflect something based on the scoring system. Some examples:

- ZAP! Another team (Their score goes to zero)
- Steal 2 points from another team
- Lose 2 points
- ZAP! All teams (All teams go to zero)
- Add 5 points to your score
- Add 2 points to another team
- Swap scores with another team etc

You will also need to prepare a set of questions. You may need more than the number of grid squares as some questions may not be answered. These questions can be about product knowledge, the business or any topic you want.

Divide the group into teams of any size you find manageable and create 2 - 4 teams. Decide which team goes first and ask them a question, if they get it right they get two points and get to pick a game card from the grid. The game cards can either be good, bad, or do nothing at all but are what you have pre created. If a team is ZAPPED! they lose all of their points. If the team answers the question incorrectly, the question is asked of the next team. You play until the appointed time is up or all your questions are gone. The team with the most points at the end is the winner

## DE-BRIEF AND REVIEW:

Hopefully the group will have enjoyed the experience.

**ASK THE GROUP:**

- Did you learn anything new?

# Quick Index of topics

**Topic categories and associated page numbers for quick selection of activities to meet a specific need:**

### Building Product / Service Knowledge

16. 20, 32, 42, 44, 62, 114, 116, 120, 128, 134, 136, 162, 186, 194, 198, 202, 206, 212

### Change

22, 38, 42, 48, 52, 56, 64, 72, 82, 90, 92, 94, 126, 152, 160, 164, 166, 170, 178, 186, 188

### Communication

16, 18, 28, 34, 36, 38, 46, 56, 60, 64, 74, 78, 82, 92, 94, 96, 98, 100, 104, 108, 114, 118, 134, 152, 154, 170, 172, 176, 194

### Creativity

12, 14, 20, 32, 36, 60, 64, 66, 76, 84, 102, 106, 116, 124, 136, 138, 158, 162, 176, 182, 190, 192, 194, 198, 206

### Customer Service

16, 28, 60, 72, 78, 98, 100, 116, 120, 126, 128

### Icebreakers / Shift Starters

12, 14, 20, 22, 24, 26, 36, 40, 42, 44, 50, 62, 64, 66, 68, 70, 76, 80, 82, 84, 86, 88, 90, 92, 104, 108, 110, 112. 114, 128, 136, 138, 140, 144, 146, 148, 150, 156, 158, 160, 162, 164, 178, 180, 194, 198, 200, 202, 204, 206, 208

### Improv / Thinking on your Feet

14, 20, 26, 32, 58, 60, 62, 66, 68, 76, 104, 106, 126, 128, 132, 136, 146, 148, 152, 154, 162, 176, 180, 182, 190, 194, 198, 200, 210

### Just for fun

18, 26, 30, 32, 36, 42, 44, 46, 50, 58, 60, 66, 68, 74, 80, 84, 88, 90, 96, 98, 102, 112, 128, 136, 142, 144, 146, 158, 160, 162, 168, 178, 182, 186, 198, 200, 206, 208, 212

## Leadership
18, 24, 34, 38, 56, 92, 94, 114, 170, 172, 184, 192

## Longer Term Activities
44, 62, 124, 168, 174, 186, 196, 206

## Organisation Values & Image
16, 36, 44, 62, 72, 92, 114, 134, 136, 138, 162, 192, 212

## Problem solving
22, 36, 52, 60, 72, 78, 82, 88, 120, 126, 128, 134, 164, 202, 210

## Review / Shift Endings
76, 82, 174, 188, 192, 200

## Sales
16, 22, 54, 62, 66, 76, 96, 98, 116, 120, 128, 132, 146, 178, 202

## Stress / Resilience
48, 62, 76, 82, 90, 114, 130, 164

## Teambuilding
12, 26, 30, 36, 40, 42, 44, 50, 58, 62, 66, 68, 70, 76, 82, 84, 86, 92, 102, 106, 110, 112, 114, 122, 124, 132, 134, 136, 138, 140, 142, 144, 148, 150, 156, 158, 162, 168, 174, 176, 180, 182, 186, 190, 192, 194, 196, 198, 204, 208

**Thank you for purchasing this book of remote activities. We trust you got a lot out of it and enjoyed the remote activities we put together for you.**

If you enjoyed this book, we are sure you will love our other activity book which has a wide range of differing activities from icebreakers, energizers, review activities, and large team activities with 101 tried and tested training activities from over 20 years of classroom training experience:

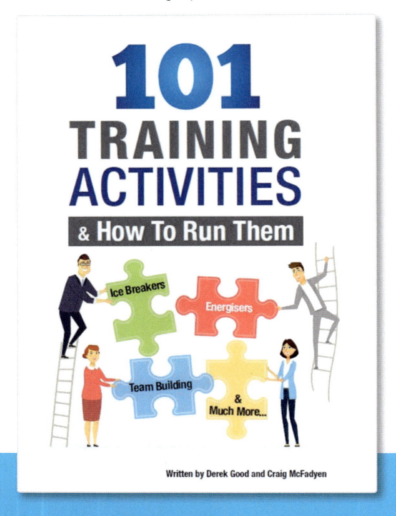

**This book is available in both hardback copy and Kindle version from Amazon:**

https://www.amazon.com/101-Training-Activities-How-Them/dp/1987708784

Manufactured by Amazon.ca
Bolton, ON